Lincoln Cent Er ... 2021

By: Stan McDonald rev02.09.2021

Preface
Welcome to the 2021 Lincoln Cent Error Coin Guide with many new photographs and error listings. The Lincoln cent error guide has more than 2,000 listings for all types of known errors.

The wide range of auction prices paid for Lincoln cent errors makes this guide a necessity for a collector evaluating encapsulating or purchasing an error coin.

Listings in this book include:
• Die errors – Errors created from broken dies, collars, and misaligned dies. DDO, DDR, cuds, die cracks, and more.
• Planchet errors – cracked, defective, lamination, clips, foreign stock, unplated, and more.
• Striking errors – Errors caused in the minting process – bonded, broadstruck, brockage, clashed dies, double struck, indent, flip over, and much more.

After 20 years, this coin guide remains unsurpassed and the most comprehensive guide available. This book provides the most authenticated coin errors by the world-leading coin experts from ANACS, PCGS, and NGC.

There are thousands of error coins in circulation. Most of the coins in circulation have minor errors such as die breaks, die cracks, and minor doubling. We have dedicated a book to these types of errors, "2021 Lincoln Cent Error - Roll Searching Guide Coin Guide."

Book Updates

New error entries and auction results are updated annually. We attend major auctions to obtain the latest values for error coins encapsulated, providing collectors credible and accurate information.

It is unclear why some error coins have a vast range of final auction prices within the same grade. Without this book, there is no official guide for the market for error coins. We have seen an error coin sell for $35 at one auction, and a similar coin selling for over $3,000. A collector armed with this guide can purchase and sell coins with confidence. This guide helps the collector pay fair market value with assurance the coin, if resold, meets the collectors' expectations.

Even with the US Mint using the best technology for producing billions of Lincoln cents, there are still modern-day errors in circulation. The wear and tear on the dies, the dies' reworking, and malfunctions in the minting process create a multitude of mint errors escaping detection.

With so many error coin listings in this book, it would be a significant challenge to add photographs for each error. Error definitions with photos in this guide show the types of errors that can occur.

Detecting a DDO or DDR coin is understanding what constitutes the error. The doubling must be the height of the typical strike or stuck over the top of the coin's intended features. The extent of the doubling on a coin is referred to as the spread. Spread has three categories, minor, medium, and wide. Thousands of coins appear doubled, but most are machine doubled.

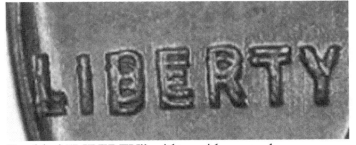

Doubled "LIBERTY" with a wide-spread.

Doubled "LIBERTY" with medium-spread. Note the doubling is created by raised lines as shown by the blue arrows.

Above is a machine doubled coin.

PCGS notes doubling as, "A die that has been struck more than once by a hub in misaligned positions, resulting in doubling of design elements. Before introducing hubbing, the individual elements of a coin's design were either engraved or punched into the die, so any doubling was limited to a specific element. With hubbed dies, multiple impressions are needed from the hub to make a single die with adequate detail. When shifting occurs in the alignment between the hub and the die, the die ends up with some of its features doubled – then imparts this doubling to every coin it strikes. The coins struck from such dies are called double-die errors – the most famous 1955 Doubled Die Lincoln cent. PCGS uses doubled die as the designation.[1]"

Searching and discovering error coins can be a rewarding and profitable experience. There are thousands of coins in circulation with various error types. Change from transactions, bankrolled coin, and looking through old collections are sources for error coin seekers.

We have included some of the known variations of coin mintages in this book. Variations of dies include coins minted with a different date placement, size of letters, numbers, and mintmark location. There are coin guides and websites dedicated to cataloging error coins and variations, such as Wexler's guide[2].

Lincoln Cent Specifications1982 - date
Composition – 2.5% Copper 97.5% Zinc
Weight – 2.5 grams
Diameter – 19.05 mm .750 in
Thickness – 1.52 mm

Pre-1982 Lincoln Cents[3]

---

[1] From the PCGS website – PCGS Lingo
[2] Wexler's guide – www.doubleddie.com
[3] 1982 was a transitional change year. Both zinc and copper types

4

Composition - .95 copper, .050 tin, and zinc
Weight – 3.11 grams
Diameter – 19.05 mm .750 in
Thickness – 1.52 mm

Distribution of coins and notes

"Currency notes and coins are all produced by the Treasury Department. After production, the Treasury ships the coins and currency notes' directly to Federal Reserve banks and branches. The Federal Reserve then releases them as required by the commercial banking system. The demand for money by the public varies from day to day and from week to week. There are even differences from season to season. Banks are usually first to feel the impact of the public's demand for cash. To meet the public's needs, banks turn to their regional Federal Reserve bank for coins and currency when their supplies are low.[4]"

"Coin Distribution, too, assures the smooth and sufficient flow of coins; the United States Mint continually revises its techniques for estimating coinage demands. In planning production and scheduling coin shipments, the United States Mint uses long-range economic indicators and historical seasonal trends such as Christmas to decide how many coins to manufacture."[5]

"Forecasting coin demand is difficult. Estimates must also include an amount enough to provide an inventory that would absorb any deviation. Armored carriers usually transport ten-cent coins, quarter-dollar coins, and half-dollar coins, while tractor-trailer trucks transport one-cent coins and five-cent coins.[6]"

---

were made for circulation.
[4] US Mint website
[5] US Mint website

"Federal Reserve banks arrange in advance to receive new coin shipments for the coming year. They do this in amounts and on a schedule to maintain their inventories at the required levels. Under this arrangement, the United States Mint can schedule its production schedule efficiently. Even with planning, there are occasions when coin shortages arise. The Federal Reserve banks must follow the advance shipping schedules. Except in an emergency, there are no provisions for obtaining additional coins.[7]"

"Federal Reserve banks receive coins at face value because they are obligations of the United States Government. The Banks store the coins until they need to fill orders from the commercial banks in their district. The Federal Reserve banks fill these orders from their vault stocks of both new and circulated coins. Also, they fill the orders without regard to date or mintmark. Coin shipments leave the Federal Reserve banks by armored car, registered mail, or express.[8]"

"If a commercial bank has excess coins on hand, they may return the coins to the Federal Reserve bank. It then sorts the coins for fitness. They return badly worn or bent coins to the United States Mint, which melts them down and makes them into new coins. Also, the banks remove foreign and counterfeit coins from circulation. According to Federal Reserve sources, over 20 billion coins valued at well over $2 billion passes through their coin processing units each year."[9]

---

[6] US Mint website
[7] US Mint website
[8] US Mint website
[9] US Mint website

Discovering an error coin

We emphasize the importance of obtaining a professional opinion about the type of error and the potential value of the error before sending it to an encapsulation service. If you believe you have an error coin, the best practice is to bring it to a certified coin dealer with an ANA and or PNG membership.

Collecting today

How do you, as a collector, obtain coinage to search? If a collector wants to search for error cents, purchasing a box of rolled cents from a bank can be rewarding. You may even find some wheat cents. Another method of searching for collectible coins is to buy a bag of wheat cents from a coin show or a coin dealer. Some dealers purchase wheat cents in bulk and do not take the time to search through the coins.

Encapsulated Coins

The primary encapsulation services use standard labeling for error coins, describing the error and the coin's grade.

The encapsulation cost, shipping, and insurance charges, of many error coins will not return the investment of certifying the coin. We cannot emphasize the importance of obtaining a professional opinion about the type of error and the potential value of the error before sending it to an encapsulation service. If you believe you have an error coin, the best practice is to bring it to a coin dealer certified as an ANA and PNG dealer to obtain an expert opinion.

Cleaning Coins

Cleaning a coin is never a good idea since it may reduce the value of the coin. Cleaning a coin with blemishes or unsightly surface flaws usually decreases the coin's value.

The encapsulation services do encapsulate coins of value with issues. NGC, PCGS, and ANACS make notations on the holder, such as "cleaned," "damaged," "holed," and "scratched" when problems are recognized.

There are no known processes or chemicals which can clean a coin without being detected. One of the most common practices to clean a coin is whizzing, using a swirling brush with high-pressure water. Whizzing shows fine lines from the brushing that can be detected.

A cleaned copper coin is usually dull, and the luster of the coin denigrates in the cleaning process. Collectors should avoid any dull copper coin or a coin with a discolored copper surface.

Index

- Die adjustment strike
- Die cap
- Die clash
- Double struck
- Fold over strike/Fold overstrike
- Indent
- Mated pair
- Mules
- Multiple struck
- Off center
- Partial collar
- Oddities
- Rotated dies
- Saddle struck
- Strike-through
- Uniface strike

Chapter Seven – Photographs of Errors

Chapter Eight – History of the Lincoln Cent and Design Changes

Glossary

References

Appendix A - Doubled Die Classifications

Appendix B - Doubled Die Classifications

Chapter One – Variations and Error Categories

Variations

Variations are not mint errors in the technical sense. Creating new hubs and dies not precisely like the original results in variations. In early U.S. coinage, there are dates of coins having multiple numbers of changes in date size, appearance, and so forth.

Some die variations are valuable, and others command no value difference between the coin variations of the same date and mintmark. Coins minted with die variations increase in value by the rarity of the number of coins minted. The rarest variety coin in the Lincoln cent collection is the 1909-S VDB.

Major Error Categories

Error coins escaping detection from the mint get bagged in the minting process. Banks and companies that have accounts with the Federal Reserve receive mint sealed bags of coins. The opening of the mint bags leads to discovering errors, especially when the coin will not fit into a roll.

Die errors - Doubled dies

Coins designated as doubled dies are the result of imperfect dies prepared from the master hub. Dies are impressed on the master hub several times to create a working die for minting coins. Doubling occurs when there is a misalignment of the impressions on the die. PCGS describes as doubled die as a die that has been struck more than once by a hub in misaligned positions, resulting in doubling of design elements.[10]

Early mintages of US coins were either engraved or punched into the die. With the advent of hubbed dies, multiple impressions are needed from the hub to make a single die with adequate detail. When shifting occurs in the alignment between the hub and the die, the die ends up with some of its features doubled – then imparts this doubling to every coin it strikes.

Doubling noted as RPM (re-punched mintmark) results from mint workers refining a mintmark by reworking a die. Most of the mintmark coin errors are RPM related.

Mint Striking Errors

Collectors and organizations dedicated to collecting coins' regard mint striking errors as those created by the mint stamping process.
The striking errors include coins struck multiple times, coins struck with a broken or loose collar, coins struck over another coin entering the minting chamber, and coins struck with flawed dies.

Planchet Error

A type I planchet is the blank itself. The blank with the edging rolled on it is a type II planchet. The kind of planchet error is essential in the classification of some error coins and their value.

Planchet errors include defective, wrong, incorrect materials. A transitional mistake results from the mint changing the planchet's alloy, and some of the replaced planchets are processed accidentally. The planchets not intended for use result are named as transitional errors.

---

[10] PCGS Website

Coin Grading

Coin grading is subjective, especially with mint state coins. Photographic coin guides providing grading by denomination help determine a coin's grade, but there is no scientific process. PCGS, NGC, and other grading services determine the methods for grading mint state coins based on a panel of experts. The experts nominate a coin for a grade, and the opinion of the majority rules the final decision.

Some coins are on the borderline between one grade and another. Dealers and grading services expand the grading for valuable coins by using more refined standards. These standards result in utilizing a coin grade with a numbering system. For example, a coin graded as Fine 12 or Fine 15 versus a grade of "fine."

The Environment

For the novice collector, it is imperative to understand the impact of the storage of coins. Coins stored in flips, not PVC free, eventually absorb the PVC. PVC destroys the original luster of a coin.

Coins stored in a moist environment degrade with oxidation and may become discolored and pitted. Coins stored in the "blue" Whitman non-acid free folders attract carbon spots, pitting, and other distractions. Carbon spotting does detract from a coin's value, and the extent of the spotting causes the coin classified as "corroded.[11]"

PCGS defines carbon spotting as "A spot seen mainly on copper and gold coins, though also occasionally found on U.S. nickel coins (which are 75 percent copper) and silver coins (which are 10 percent copper). Carbon spots are

---

[11] PCGS website

brown to black spots of oxidation ranging from minor to severe.[12]"

Best coin storage
Clean, dry place free of chemicals.
PVC, acid-free coin folders
Encapsulated

Brilliant Uncirculated
PCGS defines BU as: "A generic term applied to any coin that has not been in circulation. Sometimes applied to Lincoln cent coins with little "brilliance" left, coins not brilliant are Uncirculated.[13]"

Many sellers use "brilliant uncirculated" as a reference for brown Lincoln cents. The proper identification is "uncirculated or MS__." The most popular encapsulation services list coins as Red/Brown, Brown, or Red for Lincoln cents. MS60 designations can result from a coin with scratches, severe nicks, cleaning, or other distractions degrading the value.

Choice Uncirculated
An Uncirculated coin grading MS-63 or MS-64.

---

[12] PCGS website
[13] PCGS website

Chapter Two – Error Definitions - "BIE" errors, Doubled dies, Mint striking errors, and Planchet errors

Rev. 02.09.2021

Abrasions (die error)

Scratches on the die cause the scattered lines on the surface of a coin.

1987 Lincoln cent

1998-P Jefferson nickel

Bar Die Break (die error)

A die break over the tops of the lettering on a coin appears like a bar.

2020 Jefferson nickel

"BIE" errors (die error)

A common die break error occurred with the Lincoln cents, especially in the 1950s, with a die break. The break shows extra material between the B and the E, thus "BIE."

1992 Lincoln cent

Blank

The metal disk punched from sheet stock. A type I planchet is the metal disk without edging. A type II planchet has a rolled edge.

Type I blank   Type II blank

Bonded Pair (striking error)

Two or more blanks enter the minting chamber struck together as one piece.

1999 Lincoln cent – bonded pair

Broad strike – (striking error)

The collar holding the planchet for striking is cracked or missing creating a coin wider than usual.

Brockage – (striking error)

PCGS definition: "A brockage is a Mint error, an early capped die impression where a sharp incused image has

17

been left on the next coin fed into the coining chamber. Most brockages are partial; full brockages are rare and the most desirable form of the error.[14]"

Lincoln cent

Broken Hub (die error)
When a piece of the hub breaks off, the dies created from the hub are missing the detail.

1979 Lincoln cent

Broken Punch (die error)
A punch used to create a die is partially broken, resulting in missing details.

---

[14] PCGS website

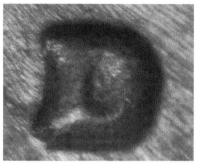
1966 Lincoln cent with missing details on the D mintmark

Canceled Planchet – (striking error)
The mint destroys coins, not meeting standards by crushing the coin. Collectors call these coins "waffle."

Canceled Jefferson nickel SMC2021

Clipped Planchets – (planchet error)
A clipped planchet error refers to many types of issues with obtaining a complete blank for minting. Many planchet errors are missing portions of the edge of the coin or most of the planchet itself. The most common error type is a planchet resulting in a half-moon.

Some of the planchet errors can be severe with various types of missing pieces. Classifications include clipped planchets, curved clips, bowtie clips, assay clips, and others.

1945 Lincoln cent

Collar Break – Vertical (die error)
A collar breaking vertically during the minting process, giving the coin a doubled rim.

1994-P Jefferson nickel – smc12.20.2020

Collar Clash (striking error)
A collar clash occurs when the striking die is not lined up correctly, and the die strikes the collar. The features on the collar, sometimes a reeded edge, is transferred to the die.

1999-D Lincoln cent

The rim is thicker on one side of the coin with a narrow rim on the 1999 photograph.

Clashed Dies – (die error)

See die clash

Counter brockages/Reverse Brockage – (striking error)

A previously struck coin and capped die is a "counter brockage." The capped die strikes a coin already struck, and the obverse design is impressed into the cap. The result will be a design where the cap face will be an incuse[15] brockage.

---

[15] Merriam-Webster - formed by stamping or punching in —used chiefly of old coins or features of their design

Counter Brockage

Debris in Hub (Hub Error)

A coin with debris in the hub transferred to a working die shows as a bold, thick line on the surface of the coin. [16]

1983 Lincoln cent — smc2021

Defective Planchet (planchet error)

A defective planchet refers to a blank which was split, cracked, or missing pieces before the coining process.

---

[16] Debris in hub - http://www.error-ref.com/

1965 Lincoln cent

Die Adjustment Strikes (striking error)
Adjustments to the pressure in the coining press results in coins weakly struck.

Die set up strike

Die Breaks (die error)
Die breaks result from a hammer or anvil die breaking. During the stamping process, the break is filled in with metal under pressure, forming raised areas on the surface of the coin.

1995 Lincoln cent smc12.19.2020

Above is a 1995 Lincoln cent with raised metal inside of the first nine.

1918-D die break rim smc02.08.2021

Die Cap – (striking error)

The term applied to an error in which a coin gets jammed in the coining press and remains for successive strikes, eventually forming a "cap" either on the upper or lower die.

Die cap error 1999 Lincoln cent – smc2019.

Die Clash – (striking error)

A coin minted with traces of the reverse on the obverse or the opposite is a "die clash" error. Die clash errors result from the minting dies pressed together without a planchet between them - one die imprints with the details of the other side of the die. In subsequent stampings, the coins minted contain some of the reverse or obverse details on opposite sides of the coin.

Lincoln cent die clash

Die Crack (die error)

The mint die incurs a fracture or break. The crack in the die fills with metal from the stamping process, leaving a raised line. The photograph shows a die crack branching in two directions.

2020 Lincoln cent – smc2020

Die Cud (die error)

A die cud occurs when part of the die breaks away, and the metal flows into the break during the minting process.

1975 Die cud – smc2020

Die Cud - retained (die error)

A retained cud occurs when a piece of the die breaks but is held in place by the collar. A retained cud may still show the coin details with raised metal flow lines.

Retained Die Cud

Die Gouges (die error)

The material in the form of short, thick, raised lines or bumps is a die gouge. Die gouges are caused by a die that has been deeply scratched or gouged by foreign material.

1986 Lincoln cent – smc12.19.2020

Two die gouges reside on the top right side of the coin in the photograph.

Die Scratches (see Abrasions)

A series of lines in different directions on the surface of the coin results from the die scratch abrasions. The abrasions could be from debris or tooling the die.

Lincoln Cent

Die Wear (die error)

Extensive die wear reduces or eliminates the details on the coin. Some collectors might mistake this coin for a strike through grease, but it is not.

Lincoln cent BU — smc10.15.2019

Doubled Die (die error)

A distinct doubling of the design on a coin created from dies doubled from the hub.

PCGS notes doubling as, "A die struck more than once by a hub in misaligned positions, resulting in doubling of design elements. Before the introduction of hubbing, the individual elements of a coin's design were either engraved or punched into the die, so any doubling was limited to a specific element. With hubbed dies, multiple impressions are needed from the hub to make a single die with adequate detail. When shifting occurs in the alignment between the hub and the die, the die ends up with some of its features doubled – then imparts this doubling to every coin it strikes. The coins struck from such dies are called doubled-die errors – the most famous being the 1955 Doubled Die Lincoln cent. PCGS uses doubled die as the designation.[17]"

1972

Double Denomination

A coin struck on another denomination previously minted.

Lincoln cent struck on a Roosevelt dime -smc02.01.2021

---

[17] From the PCGS website – PCGS Lingo

Double Struck – (striking error)
See also multiple struck.
A double-struck coin results when a coin remains in the minting chamber, then it is struck again with the dies.

1964

Extended Rim (striking error)
An extended rim occurs with a deep strike on the coin. Slight tilting of the coin during the minting process creates a thin rim with a groove inside the rim.

Filled Dies (die error)
Dies filled with metal or debris produce weakly struck coins.

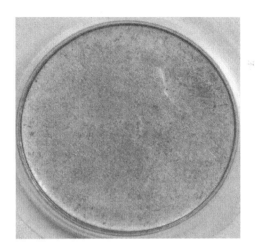

Finned Rim (striking error)

A coin minted with an extended rim missing metal fill. The fin on the rim is thin and extends part of the way around the coin.

Finned rim

Flip Over Strike (striking error)

A coin minted on one side flips over in the minting chamber and is struck again.

Flip over/double struck

Fold Over Strike– (striking error)

A coin not fully ejected in the minting chamber is struck again, crushing the coin.

No date Lincoln cent

Foreign Planchet – (planchet error)

Countries that do not have minting coin capability often request the US Mint to make coins to their specifications. Sometimes a foreign planchet makes its way into a minting chamber and is struck with US coin dies.

1998 Foreign planchet

Fragment

A fragment is a piece of metal that could be intended as scrap but was minted as a coin.

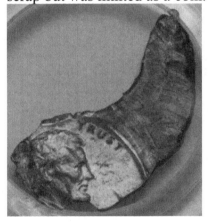

Improperly Annealed – (planchet error)

Planchets that are not properly softened for minting. The minted coins often appear with a red tint. Some flaking or missing plating may be seen on the rim of coins.

Improperly annealed

Indent – (striking error)

A recess on a coin results from one coin struck by another planchet entering the coin chamber.

Double indent – photograph courtesy of Pennies on the Dollar@pennies on the dollar (Twitter).

Inverted Mintmark (die error)

A mintmark placed on a working die upside down.

Lamination Error – (planchet error)

A piece of the planchet weakened when struck is a lamination error.

Lincoln cent

Lamination Error - Retained – (planchet error)

Retained lamination occurs when the planchet, which peels away, is intact on the surface of the coin.

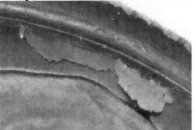

1966 BU Jefferson nickel smc1998

Machine Doubled

Machine doubling occurs in the minting process when the hammer die bounces on the surface of the coin during the strike. Machine doubling is a thin flat area surrounding the letters or numbers on the intended design.

Machine doubled

Mated Pairs – (striking error)

Two planchets struck together in error. The coins separate and are boxed in the same container. The two separate coins are located as a pair.

1999 Lincoln cents

Misaligned Dies (die error)

There are three dies, the hammer, the anvil, and the collar, designed to mint coins as intended. When the dies are not aligned correctly, the strike on the coin is not centered.

1999-D

Misplaced Date (die error)

The date is incorrectly positioned on the die.

1866 Half Dollar with wider spacing than usual.

Missing Details – (die error)

Part of the design is not transferred to the coin properly.

2000-P Roosevelt Dime – smc2000

Mule Error – (die error)

A mule error occurs when obverse details are of one coin, and the reverse is of another coin.

Lincoln cent planchet with a dime reverse.

Multiple Struck – (striking error)

A jammed coin in the coining chamber may get struck three, four, five, or more times.

Triple struck – photograph courtesy of Pennies on the Dollar@pennies on the dollar (Twitter).

Occluded Gas (planchet error)

Bubbles appear on the surface of the coin caused by gas trapped during the plating process.

1982-D

Off Center – (striking error)

A coin struck on a blank that was not properly centered over the anvil, or lower, die.[18]

Off-center

Over Mintmark (die error)

A mint worked punched another mintmark over the top of a partially removed mintmark. Subsequent mintages show a partial mintmark of the letter removed.

---

[18] PCGS – PCGS website

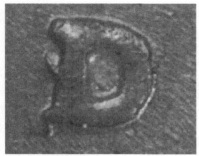

1964-D OMM

Partial Collar – (striking error)

A planchet fed into the minting chamber is stuck outside of the collar.

1918-S Lincoln cent

Partial Collar Tilted – (striking error)

A coin entering the minting chamber struck on an angle with a cracked or moving collar.

1944 Lincoln cent

Phantom Mintmark (die error)

A mintmark not completely removed from a die shows traces of the letter.

Reverse Brockage – (striking error)

Similar brockage but with the portrait facing the opposite way.

Lincoln cent

Rotated – (striking error)

The dies are not aligned correctly, leading to a rotated coin. Rotations can be slight or significant in degree.

Lincoln cent - reverse rotated – smc2015.

RPM's/RPD's/OMM's/MPD's (die error)

Re-punched mintmarks result from a mint worker repairing the die. Coin dies used before 1986 required manual rework to continue using them. An RPM is the result of repairing a mint mark and leaving traces of the die's original mint mark.

RPM

Coins discovered with dates appearing multiple times in various locations on the coin are MPD's[19] (misplaced dates).

Saddle-struck – (striking error)

Saddle struck.

Saddle struck coins occur in a multi-press operation when the coin straddles two presses. Both presses stamp the coin while the coin bends between the dies in the shape of a saddle.

Split Planchet (planchet error)

Part of the planchet is missing before striking.

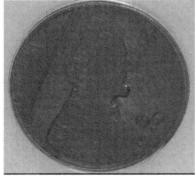

Split planchet

Spread (striking error)

[19] MPD – Missed placed date

Spread is the degree of doubling on a coin. The spread is wide, medium, or small.[20]

Doubled "LIBERTY", with a wide-spread.

Doubled "LIBERTY", with medium-spread. Note the doubling is created by raised lines as shown by the blue arrows.

---

[20] There is no standard for the nomenclature used to describe the breadth of the error.

Strike-through – (striking error)

Debris enters the minting chamber and is pressed into the coin, causing the details to be wholly or partially blurred. Extreme cases involve paper clips, staples, and other objects impressed into the coin.

Strike through

Thin/Thick Planchet (planchet error)

All US denominations have tolerances for the thickness of the coin. When a planchet is thin or thick, the coin becomes lighter or heavier than intended.

Tilted Collar (striking error)

A tilted collar strike occurs when a planchet enters the minting chamber on an angle and is struck by the hammer die pushing the coin flat. The result of this strike is a smooth outer surface lacking detail.

1913 Buffalo Nickel

Tilted Mintmark (die error)

A mintmark hammered into a die at an angle, leaving the details thick on one side and thin on the other side.

Lincoln cent – S tilted

Transitional – (planchet error)

A transitional error refers to minting a coin on discontinued planchet stock from the prior year. Examples are a 1983 Lincoln cent minted on a copper planchet and a 1943 cent minted on a copper planchet.

Uniface – (striking error)

A coin planchet enters the minting chamber over a planchet already in the minting chamber. The planchets struck together, resulting in one side blank and the other side with the intended details.

Uniface Lincoln cent

Unplated – (planchet error)

A coin missing the plating layer exposing the inner core.

1983 Lincoln cent with no copper plating[21] The coin appears zinc colored.

Wrong Metal – (planchet error)

A metal alloy unintentionally used for the minting of coins such as brass.

Discoveries of brass cents are dated 1983, 1983-D, 1989-D, and 1990-D. Regular copper-coated zinc coins weigh

---

[21] Located by the author in a stash of cents.

around 2.5 grams versus a brass or copper cent weighing 3.11 grams.

Wrong Planchet – (planchet error)

A coin struck on a different planchet than intended is considered a wrong planchet.

1963-D Lincoln cent struck on a dime planchet.

Chapter Three – Lincoln Die Cent Errors

- Filled letters/numbers (BIE errors)
- Die cracks
- Die cuds
- Doubled dies
- Missing details (no FG, letters, numbers, and other details)
- Close and wide AM – Proof dies used for standard mintages

No other coin series has as many error coins as the Lincoln cent series. The vast number of one-cent coins minted, and the dies' reworking have created thousands of DDO and DDR errors. The number of errors and variations are numerous, and discoveries will continue as collectors search through their coins.

Below is the grading number system for the services and people who catalog Lincoln cent coin errors:
Fivaz Stanton: Old FS-1-016 New FS-01-1936-103
Breen: 2135
Coneca: 3-O-V
Crawford: CDDO-003
Wexler: WDDO-003.

PCGS uses the FS designation or no designation to classify coin errors. NGC uses the FS standard and VarietyPlus - VP-xxx. "The VarietyPlus service was launched by NGC in 1996 to provide accurate attribution services for US coin varieties. A variety is a coin that is distinguished by characteristics specific to the dies that struck it.[22]" ANACS uses all designations.

---

[22] NGC website

BIE Errors
1953-D (MS63, $15) 2020
1954-S (MS63, $11) (MS64, $15-$40) (MS66, $26-$29) 2020
1955-D (MS66, $3.45) 2020
1955-S (MS65, $17) (MS66, $21-$32) 2020
1992 (MS60, $9) 2020

Die Cracks
1918 die crack (F12, $70) 2018
1922 die crack weak reverse (AU53, $978) 2020
1922-D die crack reverse (MS63, $212) 2020
1955-S die crack (MS65, $47-$70) 2020
1999 die crack obverse (MS60, $70) 2020

Die Cuds
1943-S reverse (MS67, $50) 2020
1970-S LD obverse (MS63, $47) 2020
1972-D obverse (MS65, $441) 2020
1973-D obverse (MS65, $403) (MS66, $441) 2020
1975-D obverse (MS64, $54) 2020

Below is a long list of error coins with the PCGS, NGC, and ANACS encapsulated grades and ranges of prices from completed auctions. Dates below not labeled as DDO or DDR are RPM's.

Doubled Dies - DDO, DDR and other Doubled Errors
1909 VDB DDO[23] (F15, $55) (XF40, $80) (XF45, $74) (AU55, $56-$85) (recolored, AU55, $55) (AU58, $97-$325) (MS60, $80) (MS60, recolored, $115) (MS61, $125-$149) (MS62, $34-$545) (MS63, $43-$210) (MS64, $40-$1,840)

---

[23] Die 1 and Die 2 no significant value differences

(MS65, $100-$5,750) (MS66, $747-$12,075) (MS67, $12,000-$24,150) 2020 photo
1909 VDB DDR (MS64, $120) 2017
1909-S S/horizontal S (AG3, corroded, $35) (G6, $65-$70) (scratched, G6, $55) (VG8, $80-$98) (VG10, $74-$110) (VG10, scratched, cleaned, $85) (VG10, rim damage, $85) (F12, $74-$160) (F12, cleaned, $74-$127) (F12, corroded, $65) (F12, environmental damage, $55-$60) (F15, $75-$95) (F15, cleaned, $109) (VF20, $90-$138) (VF20, corroded, scratched, $90-$100) (VF20, environmental damage, $50)) (VF20, scratched, $85-$152) (VF25, $96-$138) (VF30, $75-$130) (VF30, cleaned , $103) (VF30, corroded, $115) (VF30, scratched, $90-$95) (VF35, $105-$184) (XF40, $122-$160) (XF40, cleaned, $135) (XF40, damaged, $89) (XF40, scratched, $135) (XF45, $75-$190) (XF45, corroded, $90-$120) (XF45, scratched, $138) (AU50, cleaned, $153-$160) (AU50, cleaned, corroded, $103) (AU55, $110-$130) (MS60, recolored, $155) (MS61, $120-$127) (MS62, $127) (MS63, $299-$345) (MS64, $518) (MS65, $1,006) (MS66, $2,070) 2020 photo
1910-S S/S (VF30, $66-$70) (VF35, $35-$45) (AU55, cleaned, $68) (MS60, $75) (MS64, $515-$662) (MS65, $268-$1,725) (MS66, $1,750-$1,800) 2020 photo
1911-D D/D (VF25, $105) (XF40, $125) (AU53, $495) (AU58, $500) 2017 photo
1911-S S/S (VF25, $100) (AU55, $175-$180) (AU58, $153) (MS61, $160-$165) (MS62, $159-$245) (MS63, $195-$350) (MS64, $617) (MS65, $950-$1320) 2020 photo
1912-S S/S (XF40, $50) (AU58, $153) (MS62, $159-$635) (MS63, $200) 2018 photo
1917 DDO (G4 $69-$185) (VG8, $140-$195), (VG10, $160) (F12 $144) (VF20, $280) (AU 55, $1925-$2040) (MS65, $8,700-$13,800) (MS66, $25,300-$28,750) 2020 photo
1922 no D or partial D (G6, $250) (VG8, $800) (AU55, $4,100) (MS63, $2,500-$14,000) photo

1924-S S/S (AU50, $94) 2020
1925-S DDO (VF30, $15-$20) (MS60, $375) (MS65, $1,116-$1,125) 2019
1925-S S/S (F15, $12-$50) (VF30, $16) (VF35, $16) (XF45, $75) (AU55, $35) (MS62, $70-$76) (MS63, 376) (MS65, $1,100) 2020 photo
1927 D/D (VF20, $19) (MS64, $660-$3,300) 2018 photo
1927 DDO (VF25, $99-$165) (AU50, $42-$180) (MS65, $525) 2020 photo
1928-S Large S (MS63, $120) (MS64, $500-$1,320) (MS65, $1,560) 2020 photo
1929-S S/S (MS65, $1,060-$2,600) (MS66, $2,700-$2,900) 2019 photo
1930-S S/S (MS63, $300) (MS64, $80-$170) (MS66, $225) 2019 photo
1932-D DDO (AU50, $20) (MS64, $115) 2018
1934 DDO (MS65, $445-$1,035) 2018 photo
1934-D DDO (MS64, $51-$70) 2018
1934-D/D (F12, $55) (MS65, $445) 2018 photo
1935 DDO (XF40, $45-$50) (MS63, $248) (MS64, $375) (MS65, $26-$440) 2018 photo
1935 DDR (VF35, $250-$255) (MS67, $200) 2018
1936 DDO die 1 (genuine, $55) (F12, $90) (VF35, $144) (XF45, $95-$185) (AU85, $222) (MS62, $545-$646) (MS63, $1,400-$4,025) (MS64, $2,585-$5,175) (MS65, $7,050-$10,925) (MS66, $11,500-$21,850) 2020 photo
1936 DDO die 2 (VF30, $170) (XF40, $75-$110) (XF45, $100-$185) (MS60, $1,610) (MS62, $370-$375) (MS63, $140-$330) (MS64, $423-$1,840) (MS65, $485-$3,565) (MS66, $12,820-$8,050) (PR62, $200) (PR64, $390) (PR65, $1,260-$1,980) (PR66, $2,400) 2020 photo
1936 DDO die 3 (scratched XF40, $40) (MS64, $245-$250) (MS65, $376-$1,700) (MS66, $690-$1,140) 2020 photo
1936 DDO die 4 (MS65, $105) 2017
1936 DDO proof type (PR62, $195), (PR65, $600-$1560) (PR66, $5,400-$5,750) 2020

1936 DDR (MS64, $25) (MS65, $25-$105) (MS66, $130)
2018
1937 DDR (MS64, $10-$15) 2018 photo
1938 DDR (MS65, $90) 2017
1938-D D/D (MS65, $21-$40) 2014 photo
1938-D DDR (MS65, $20) 2018
1938-S S/S (VF25, $112) (AU58, $30-$35) (MS64, $31-
$125) (MS65, $26-$300) (MS66, $30-$260) (MS67, $110-
$260) 2019 photo
1938-S Triple S (MS63, $95) (MS64, $55-$60) (MS65,
$21-$129) (MS66, $39-$120) (MS67, $100-$135) 2019
photo
1939 DDO (MS62, $84) (MS64, $120-$132) (MS65, $250-
$312) (MS66, $255-$960) 2020 photo
1939 DDR (MS64, $121) 2018
1939-S S/S (MS65, $30) 2016 photo
1940-D D/D (MS64, $23) 2014 photo
1940-S DDR (MS66, $65) 2018 photo
1940-S S/S (MS63, $45-$50) (MS64, $65-$110) (MS65,
$70-$355) (MS66, $40-$275) (MS67, $125-$130) 2019
photo
1940-S Triple S (MS64, $26-$79) (MS66, $58-$132) 2018
photo
1941 DDO die 1 (XF45, $89-$115) (AU55, $170) (MS63,
$215-$220) (MS64, $164-$1,998) (MS65, $822-$2,185)
(MS66, $1,525-$7,190) 2020 photo
1941 DDO die 2 (XF45, $52-$240) (AU55, $324) (AU58,
$80-$180) (MS60, $135-$140) (MS64, $350-$1,006)
(MS65, $705) (MS66, $3,525-$7,475) 2020
1941 DDO die 3 (AU53, $99) (MS65, $940) (MS66,
$8,280-$9,200) 2020
1941-D DDR (MS65, $32) (MS66, $37-$80) 2018
1941-S DDR Class VI (MS65, $38-$65) (MS66, $37-$70)
(MS67, $100) 2018
1941-S S/S (MS66, $48) 2018 photo
1942 DDO (EF45, $38) (AU50, $19) (MS67, $115) 2018

1942-D D/D (MS65, $300) (MS66, $460) 2015 photo
1942-D DDO (MS66, $28) 2018
1942-S DDO (MS64, $173-$177) (MS65, $184-$300)
(MS66, $950-$1,150) 2020
1942-S DDR (MS63, $146)
1942-S S/S (EF45, $77) (MS65, $31) (MS66, $38-$750)
(MS67, $86-$225) 2018 photo
1942-S S/S DDO (MS62, $40-$42)
1942-S Triple S DDO (MS64, $160) (MS65, $345), (MS66,
$546) (MS66, $288-$840) (MS67, $432) 2018
1943 DDO (AU50, $11) (MS63, $575) (MS64, $135-$415)
(MS65, $305-$675) (MS66, $195) 2018 photo
1943 DDO/DDR (MS64, $85-$259) (MS65, $80-$175)
(MS66, $152-$185) 2017
1943 DDR (MS62, $3-$30) 2018
1943-D repunched D minor (MS66, $140) 2020
1943-D D/D (MS64, $360-$720) (MS65, $660- $2,530)
(MS67, $4,500-$21,275) 2020
1943-D DDO (MS62, $13-$16) 2020 photo
1943-D DDR (MS64, $45) (MS65, $65) 2018
1943-S DDO (AU58, $13) (MS65, $470-$555) (MS66,
$580-$1,058) (MS67, $1,560-2,325) 2020
1943-S DDR (MS61, $6) (MS64, $42-$67) (MS65, $34)
(MS67, $435) 2018
1944 DDR (MS64, $32) (MS65, $60-$65) 2018
1944-D D/D (VF35, $20-$80) (AU58, $47) (MS60, $11-
$22), (MS64, $95-$100) (MS65, $80-$125) photo (MS66,
$81-$200) (MS67, $432-$2300) 2020
1944-D D/S (VF30 $100) (VF35, $40) (XF45, $100-$155)
(AU50, $135) (AU55/58, $140-$205) (MS60, $250) (MS63,
$125-$180) (MS64, $145-$780) (MS65, $400-$5,463)
(MS66, $720-$16,100) (MS67, $8,400) 2020 photo
1944-D DDR (MS65, $42-$184) (MS66, $60) 2018
1944-D with S located below the D ($29)
1945 DDO (MS64, $52-$435) (MS65, $14-$60) 2018
photo

1945-D D/D (MS60, $25) 2014
1945-D DDO (MS63, $37) (MS64, $30-$150) (MS65, $14)
2018
1945-S DDO (MS67, $167) photo
1945-S S/S (MS66, $150) 2016
1946 DDR (MS64, $15) (MS66, $53) 2018
1946-D D/D (MS64, $65) (MS65, $60) (MS66, $75)
(MS67, $75-$285) 2018 photo
1946-S Inverted Mint Mark (MS64, $126-$200) (MS65,
$155-$255) 2020 photo
1946-S DDO (MS65, $45-$50) (MS66, $31) (MS67, $165)
2017 photo
1946-S S/D (XF45, $130) (AU55, $60) (MS62, $103-$800)
(MS63, $150-$340) (MS64, $315-$375) (MS65, $312-
$1,880) (MS66, $1,320-$3,050) (MS67, $425) 2020 photo
1946-S S/S (MS63, $40) (MS64, $24-$37) (MS65, $27-$60)
(MS66, $29) 2018 photo
1947 DDO (MS62, $348) (MS63, $95) (MS64, $18-$345)
(MS65, $305) (MS66, $700-$1,300) (MS67, $3,055) 2020
photo
1947-S S/S (MS64, $16-$125) (MS65, $32 -$100) (MS66,
$23-$225) (MS67, $525-$780) 2020 photo
1948-S S/S (MS66, $69) 2016 photo
1948-S S/S DDO (MS65, $53-$173) 2018
1949-D D/D (MS64, $75-$95) (MS65, $300-$415) 2018
1949-S DDO (MS64, $120) (MS65, $14-$336) (MS66,
$70-$145) 2018 photo
1949-S S/S (MS65, $27-$75) 2018 photo
1950 DDR (MS65, $65-$70) (MS66, $145-$150) 2018
1950-S S/S (F15, $11) (MS62, $15) (MS65, $35-$41)
(MS66, $21-$78) 2016 photo
1951 DDO (PR63, $45) (PR64, $54-$95) (PR65, $41-$142)
(PR66, $190-$405) (PR67, $400-$4,560) (PR68, $305)
2020
1951 DDR (MS68, $50) (PR65, $50) 2018

1951-D D/D (AU58, $12) (MS64, $31) (MS65, $69-$215) 2018 photo
1951-D D/S (MS64, $55-$185) (MS65, $118) (MS66, $165-$865) (MS67, $2,350) 2014 photo
1951-D DDO (MS63, $18-$45) (MS64, $51) (MS65, $119-$152) (PR64, $75) 2020 photo
1951-D D/D/D (MS64, $75)
1952-D D/D (MS65, $15) 2016 photo
1952-D D/S (MS64, $100-$160) (MS65, $94-$264) (MS66, $525-$865) 2020 photo
1952-S S/S (MS67, $89-$117) 2018
1953 DDO (MS65, $109) (PR64, $85-$100) (PR65, $48-$60) (PR66, $70-$900) (PR67, $100-$1,300) (PR68, $1,880-$2,000) 2020
1953 DDR (PR65, $150) (PR66, $85) 2017
1953 Re-Engraved Design (PR66, $89) 2010
1953-D D/D (MS60, $14) (MS64, $25-$35) (MS65, $22-$85) (MS66, $36) 2018 photo
1953-S S/S (MS64, $85) (MS65, $28-$90) 2016 photo
1954-D D/D (MS64, $22-$65) (MS65, $69-$350) 2018 photo
1954-D D/D/D (MS64, $65) (MS65, $125-$325) (MS66, $50-$55) 2018 photo
1954-S S/S (MS64, $14-$36) (MS65, $28-$69) (MS66, $16-$22) (MS67, $65-$70) 2018 photo
1955 DDO (XF45, $700-$1,700) (AU55, $1,440) (AU58, $750-$2,100) (MS62, $1,700-2,400) (MS63, $2,000-$5,175) (MS64, $2,100-$5,400) (MS66, $1,140) 2020
1955 DDR (MS65, $30-$60) (PR62, $18) (PR66, $50-$120) (PR67, $67) 2018 photo
1955 DDR and DDO (PR65, $25-$125) (PR66, $25-$70) 2019
1955-D D/D (MS64, $17) (MS65, $22-$115) (MS66, $23-$145) 2018 photo
1955-D D/S (MS65, $90) 2017

1955-D DDO (MS64, $34-$110) (MS65, $32-$155) (MS66, $25-$405) 2020 photo
1955-D DDR (MS66, $195-$200) 2018
1955-S Filled 5 (MS65, $42-$49) 2017
1955-S S/S (MS63, $48) (MS64, $23-$92) (MS65, $42-$127) (MS66, $25-$60) 2018
1955-S S/S/S (MS64, $32-$92) (MS65, $42-$488) (MS66, $25-$306) (MS67, $79) 2018 photo
1956 DDR (MS64, $15) 2018
1956-D D/D (MS63, $90) (MS65, $35-$185), (MS66, $180-$265), (MS67, $1,293) 2020 photo
1956-D D/D/D (MS65, $59-$184) 2011
1956-D D/D/S (MS62, $180-$185) (MS64, $35-$64) (MS65, $30-$120) (MS66, $40-$250) 2018
1956-D D/S (MS64, $45-$95) (MS65, $40-$288) (MS66, $50-$1,725) 2018
1957-D D/D (MS64, $10-$32) (MS65, $29-$100) (MS66, $85) 2018 photo
1957-D D/D/D (MS65, $80) 2008 photo
1957-D DDO (MS66, $32) 2018
1958 DDO (MS64, $58,500) extremely rare[24] photo
1958 DDR (PR64, $31) 2018
1958-D D/D (MS64, $11-$21) (MS65, $11) (MS66, $32) 2018
1958-D D/D/D (MS65, $100) (MS66, $32) 2016
1958-D DDO (MS64, $11) 2018
1959 DDO (MS62, $14) (MS63, $110) (MS64, $21-$160) (MS65, $125-$280), (MS66, $600-$825) 2018 photo
1959-D D/D/D (MS63, $22-$154) (MS64, $43-$69) (MS65, $24-$184) (MS66, $30-$116) 2018 photo
1960 DDO large over small date (PR66, $193-$432) (PR67, $245-$575), (PR68, $440-$1,006), (PR69, $7,475)

---

[24] PCGS - https://www.pcgs.com/news/1958-doubled-die-lincoln-cent-remains-elusive

1960 DDO small over large date (PR65, $299-$400) (PR66, $230-$470) (PR67, $342-$530), (PR68, $1,320-$4,600) 2020
1960 DDO small over large date triple DDO (PF67, $288) 2020
1960 large date DDR (MS66, $50-$125) 2018
1960-D D/D DDO small over large date (AU50, $65) (MS62, $21) (MS63, $37-$50) (MS65, $340- $655) (MS66, $265) 2020
1960-D D/D large date (AU50, $21) (MS64, $9-$65) (MS65, $11-$70) (MS66, $60-$69) 2018 photo
1960-D D/D large over small date (MS63, $17-$46) (MS64, $9), (MS65, $20) (MS66, $676) 2018
1960-D D/D small date (MS65, $30-$220) 2018
1960-D D/D small over large date (AU50, $33) (MS61, $35) (MS62, $70-$75) (MS63, $75-$255) (MS64, $25-$322) (MS65, $90-$1,150) (MS66, $645-$4,025) 2020 photo
1960-D DDO large over small date (PR64, $109) (PR65, $138-$219) (PR66, $161-253) (PR67, $240-490) (PR68, $480-$545) 2020
1960-D DDO small over large date (PR66, $276) (PR67, $200-$260) 2020
1961 DDO (PR66, $13-$50) 2018 photo
1961-D D/D (MS63, $55-$84) (MS64, $10-$32) (MS65, $32-$105) 2018
1961-D D/D large D (MS65, $103) 2018
1961-D over Horizontal D (MS63, $60) (MS64, $21-$50) (MS65, $75-$120) (MS66, $135) 2020 photo
1962 DDO (PR66, $15-$37) 2018 photo
1963 DDO (MS65, $22) 2018
1963 DDR (MS65, $22) 2018
1963-D DDO (MS64, $22-$38) (MS65, $300-$306) 2018 photo
1964 DDO (MS64, $10-$45) 2018

1964 DDR (MS61, $12) (MS62, $34), (MS63, $105)
(MS64, $11-$150) (MS65, $99-$280), (MS66, $45-$376)
2018
1964 SMS (MS67, $11,500)
1966 DDO (AU58, $25)
1967 DDO (MS60, $47) 2015
1968-D D/D (MS63, $22) (MS65, $38-$165) 20   18
photo
1968-S DDO (MS64, $19-$121) (MS65, $90-$95) (MS66,
$185) (PR66, $94-$190) (PR67, $195-$260) (PR68, $515-
$520) 2018 photo
1968-S DDR (PR68, $525) 2017
1969-S DDO (XF45, $7,635) (AU53, $18,200-$23,000)
(AU55, $15,500-$54,625) (AU58, $7,185-$44,862) (MS60,
$20,400) (MS61, $27,600-$39,600) (MS62, $26,400-
$43,700) (MS63, $38,400-$86,250), (MS64, $36,800-
126,500) 2020 photo
1970-S DDO large date - note: variations of the degree of
error are noted with FS-101 and FS103. (MS63, FS-101,
$1,890) (MS63 FS-101, $5,750) (MS64 FS-101, $2,160-
$10,500) (MS64 FS-103, $99-$145) (MS65 FS-101,
$3,500-$9,988) (MS65 FS-103, $79) (MS66 FS-103, $435)
(PR64, $104) (PR65, $110-$225) (PR66, $110-$200)
(PR67, $185-$215) 2020
1970-S DDO small date (MS63, $24) (MS66, $105) (MS67,
$370) (PR64, $120) (PR66, $85-$90) (PR68, $360-$2,050)
2020
1970-S DDO large date (MS65, $2,640) 2020 photo
1970-S large date over small date, DDO (PR67 cameo,
$432) 2018
1970-S S/S large date (MS63, $74) (MS64, $26- $38) 2016
1970-S S/S proof (PR65, $250) 2017
1971 DDO (MS62, $94) (MS63, $160-$264) (MS64, $130-
$634) (MS65, $720-$5,465)) (MS66, $10,500) 2020 photo

1971-S DDO (PR64, $125-$290) (PR65, $95-$435) (PR66, $100-$700) (PR67, $310-$865) (PR68, $1,440-$1,645) 2020 photo
1971-S S/S (MS64, $42-$427) (MS65, $26-$431) (MS67, $5,400-$5,750) (PR65, $402-$545) (PR67, $660) (PR68, $1,645-$2,280) 2020 photo
1972 72/72 (MS63, $140-$175) (MS64, $59-$460) (MS65, $125-$662) (MS66, $630-$1,840) (MS67, $2,185-$6,470) 2018 photo
1972 DDO doubling « In God We Trust » Date » Liberty (MS60, $12-$160) (MS62, $15-$260) (MS63, $14-$336) (MS64, $42-$410) (MS65, $26-$492) (MS66, $720-$1,560) (MS67, $2,225-$14,400) 2020 photo
1972-D D/D (MS66, $27) 2016
1972-S DDO (PR64, $50-$155) (PR65, $35-$65) (PR66, $230-$1,560) 2020
1979-S Clear S (PR70, $1,400) 2017
1980 DDO (MS60, $55) (MS63, $185), (MS64, $125-$285), (MS65, $235-$250) 2018 photo
1980-D D/S (MS65, $50-$140) (MS66, $135-$405) 2018
1981-S type 1 filled S (PR70, $125-$960) 2020 photo
1981-S type 2 clear S (PR69, $100-$185) 2017
1982 DDO large date copper
1982 DDO large date die 2 (MS64, $84) (MS65, $21) 2018
1982 DDO small date copper
1982-D DDO large date copper photo
1982-D DDO small date zinc/copper plated
1982-D DOO large date zinc/copper plated
1982-D small date Bronze (AU58, $8,400) 2020
1983 DDO (MS60, $192) (MS62, $46-$110) (MS63, $74-$145) (MS64, $42-$547) (MS65, $55-$325), (MS66, $250-$865) (MS67, $500-$2,350) 2020 photo
1983 DDR (AU55, $57) (AU58, $100-$110) (MS60, $35-$159) (MS61, $105-$110) (MS62, $105-$125) (MS63, $120-$195), (MS64, $50-$245) (MS65, $235-$425) (MS66,

$305-$600) (MS67, $430-$3,650) (MS68, $2,350-$3,220)
2020 photo
1983-D DDO (MS64, $14) 2018
1984 DDO (AU58, $75-$100) (MS60, $132) (MS63, $145)
(MS64, $155-$200) (MS65, $156-$165) (MS66, $155-$330)
(MS67, $195-$600) 2020 photo
1984 DDO double ear (MS60, $90-$170) (MS62, $51-$150)
(MS63, $100-$180) (MS64, $101-$288) (MS65, $105-$325)
(MS66, $130-$823) (MS67, $190-$1,530) (MS68, $345-
$3,910) 2020 photo
1984-D D/D (MS64, $188) 2017
1984-D DDO (AU55, $74) (MS64, $185-$190) (MS67,
$345) 2018
1986 DDO (MS65, $25-$30) 2018
1987 DDO (MS64, $13-$15) 2018
1988 DDO (MS64, $14) 2018
1988-D DDO (MS64, $13-$15) (MS66, $16) 2018
1994 DDR (MS63, $70-$105) (MS64, $79-$185) (MS65,
$105-$990) (MS66, $820-$825) 2018 photo
1995 DDO (MS60, $35-$40) (MS63, $25-$45) (MS64, $42)
(MS65, $23-$145) (MS66, $21-$150) (MS67, $40-$180)
(MS68, $79- $960) (MS69, $3850) 2020 photo
1995-D DDO (AU58, $110-$115) (MS64, $380-$822)
(MS65, $432-$558) (MS67, $265-$4,200) (MS68, $80)
(MS69, $1,980) 2020 photo
1996 DDO (MS61, $89) 2015
1997 double ear (MS65, $105-$180) (MS65, $152-$196)
photo
1998-S DDO and rotated (PR69, $4,560) 2020
2006 DDO (MS65, $50-$225) 2018 photo
2014 DDO (MS64, $150) 2016
2018 DDO (MS66, $200) 2018

Missing details (no FG, letters, numbers, and other details)
1968-S No S (PR67, $18000) 2020

1969-D no FG (AU55, $35) (MS63, $63-$104) (MS65, $500) 2018

1990 no S proof (PR65, $2115) (PR66, $2,340-$5,750) (PR67, $2,500-$4,250) (PR68, $2,640-$4,990) (PR69, $3,480-$8,500) 2020

2000 missing last zero (MS60, $3) 2020

Close and wide AM – Proof dies used for standard mintages

1992 close AM (MS62, $4,800) 2020

1992-D close AM (AU55 corrosion, $455) (AU58, $960-$2,115) (MS65, $4,320) (MS66, $12,000) 2020 photo

1998 wide AM (MS65, $50) (MS66, $60-$120) (MS67, $505) 2020

1998-D proof dies (MS67, $33)

1998-S close AM (MS66, $125) (PR65, $105) (PR67, $94) (PR68, $1,265) (PR69, $235-$1,400) (PR70, $2,200-$7,400) 2020

1999 wide AM (MS64, $114-$135) (MS65, $155-$300) 2020

1999-S close AM (PR65, $29-$105) (PR67, $50-$170) (PR68, $60-$200), (PR69, $115-$1050) 2020

2000 wide AM (MS67, $156) 2020

2008 reverse of proof (MS64, $50)

Chapter Four – Lincoln Cent Off center

Note: Early encapsulations did not list the percent off center.

No date wheat cent (MS62, $92) (MS65, $12-$150) (MS66, $14- $150)

No date Memorial cent (MS60, $11-$35) (MS62, $21-$130) (MS63, $16-$25) (MS64, $23)

No date Memorial cent 50% off center (MS63, $42) 2020

1909 50% - (MS67, $44)

1910 (XF45, $115-$130)

1911 (VF25, $242) (XF45, $69-$127)

1912 (AU53, $405) (AU58, $196)

1912-D (MS63, $242)

1913 (MS60, $110) (MS63, $345-$550)

1913-D (AU55, $145) (MS60, $145)

1913-S (AU55, $435) (MS61, $825)

1914 (XF45, $66-$185) (MS60, $105) (MS64, $322)

1915 (F15, $69)

1915-D (F15, $345) (MS62, $259-$489) (MS63, $230) (MS64, $288)

1915-S AU50, $765)

1916-D (MS61, $150) (MS63, $210-$690) (MS64, $235) (MS65, $345-$550)

1916-S (MS64, $210) (MS65, $633)

1917 (G4, $47 - $55) (VF20, $56) (AU58, $253 $920) (MS63, $126) (MS64, $105-$357) (MS65, $282)

1917-D (VG8, $52) (VF30, $161) (XF40, $242) (MS60, $167) (MS63, $208 - $403) (MS64, $235-$253)

1917-S (VF20, $130 - $150) (XF45, $75-$197) (AU50, $110 - $805) (AU55, $127-$276) (AU58, $220) (MS61, $104-$276) (MS62, $207) (MS63, $547) (MS64, $576)

1918 (F12, $21) (VF30, $127-$196) (AU58, $748) (MS65, $1,725)

1918-D (MS61, $92-$150) (MS62, $99-$173) (MS64, $805)

1918-S (VF20, $133) (AU50, $161-$223) (MS62, $348) (AU58, $311) (MS60, $243-$374) (MS62, $432-$764) (MS64, $403)

1919 (AU50, $42) (MS62, $64-$265) (MS61, $184) (MS62, $138-$1,410) (MS63, $66-$218) (MS64, $92-$161)

1919-D (AU50, $35-$299)

1919-S (VG10, $51) (F12, $58-$84) (VF20, $25-$45) (VF35, $99) (XF45, $46) (AU55, $56-$374) (AU58, $86) (MS60, $141) (MS63, $92-$647) (MS64, $299-$588) (MS65, $520)

1920 (VF20, $60) (XF40, $161) (XF45, $45-$50) (AU55, $69) (MS63, $360) (MS64, $64-$375) (MS65, $288)

1920-D (AU55, $207) (XF45, $423) (MS64, $423)

1921 (VG8, $78) (MS62, $207) (MS64, $202)

1922 10% off center (XF40, $4,310-$5,290)

1924 (MS65, $80)

1924-S (AU50, $276-$547) (MS62, $705) (MS65, $1,765)

1925-D (AU50, $161)

1926-D (F15, $59) (VF25, $64) (MS64, $288)

1928-D (XF45, $63 - $99)

1929-D (MS63, $431)

1929-S (MS66, $647)

1930-D (MS62, $74)

1934 (VG10, $50)

1936 (MS64, $121)

1937(VF20, $161) (MS64, $95-$150)

1939 (AU50, $65) (MS62, $127) (MS64, $207)

1940-S (MS60, $69) (MS62, $161) (MS63, $161)

1941 (MS65, $37)

1942 (AU58, $69) (MS60, $27) (MS62, $2,585) (MS63, $35) (MS66, $92)

1943 (AU50, $42-$92) (AU55, $276) (AU58, $69-$130) (MS60, $54) (MS62, $276-$1,410) (MS63, $104-$212) (MS64, $74-$200) (MS65, $432)

1943-D (AU50, $84) (MS67, $1,610-$1,998)

1943-S (F12, $46) (VF20, $31) (VF30, $54) (XF40, $19-$75) (AU58, $104) (MS60, $42-$81) (MS62, $219-$441) (MS63, $184-$460) (MS64, $81-$423)

1944 (XF40, $12) (AU50, $10-$24) (AU53, $11) (AU55, $58) (AU58, $18-$30) (MS62, $45) (MS63, $31-$69) (MS64, $25-$165) (MS65, $66)

1944-S (MS64, $69) (MS65, $79)

1945 (XF40, $57) (XF45, $92) (MS60, $11-$61) (MS63, $34-$92) (MS64, $44 - $92) (MS65, $57) (MS67, $173 - $300)

1945-D (MS64, $42)

1945-S (AU53, $87) (MS62, $50)

1946 (MS66, $149)

1946-S (AU58, $17-$87) (MS66, $259)

1947-S (MS61, $156)

1949 (MS63, $345) (MS65, $489)

1949-D (MS64, $329)

1949-S (MS64, $253)

1950-D (AU50, $38) (MS62, $51-$60) (MS63, $29-$104) (MS64, $51 -$141)

1951 (MS60, $69) (MS63, $81-$92) (MS64, $104)

1951-D (MS60, $12-$35) (MS62, $59) (MS63, $21-$37) (MS64, $31- $242)

1952 (MS62, $59-$65) (MS63, $59-$89)

1952-D (AU58, $15-$94) (MS60, $13-$18) (MS61, $24-$51) (MS63, $24-$100) (MS64, $29-$112) (MS65, $92)

1952-S (AU58, $23) (MS64, $161)

1953 (MS60, $13) (MS64, $75-$161)

1953 70% (MS64, $505) 2020

1953-x (MS62, $36)

1953-D (MS60, $75) (MS64, $48) (MS65, $173)

1954 15%, 15% double clip (MS65, $335) 2020

1954-D 55% (MS62, $130) 2020

1954-S 5% (MS60, $40) 2020

1955 50% (AU50 cleaned, $100) 2020

1955-D (MS63, $60)

1955-D 60% (MS65, $240) 2020
1955-S 5% (MS64, $110) 2020
1955-S 10% (MS63, $87) 2020
1956 (MS63, $51)
1956 25% (MS62, $120) 2020
1956-D (MS60, $18) (MS62, $33) (MS63, $35-$192)
(MS64, $42-$253) 2019
1956-D (MS63, $105) 2020
1956-x (MS63, $37)
1957 (MS63, $37) (MS64, $88)
1957 10%, 32% straight clip (MS65, $240) 2020
1957-D (AU58, $150-$242) (MS62, $69) (MS63, $39-$54)
(MS64, $115-$218) (MS65, $127)
1957-D 60% (MS64, 200) 2020
1958 (MS63, $63-$432) 2019
1958 20% (MS63, $300) 2020
1958-D (AG3, $110) (MS63, $184-$276) (MS64, $103-
$276) (MS65, $374) (MS66, $141)
1958-D 60% (MS64, $312) 2020
1958-D 75% (MS66, $145) 2020
1959 (MS63, $81)
1959 off center, split planchet (MS64, $94)
1959 20% (MS65, $290) 2020
1959-D (MS60, $63)
1959-D 75% (MS64, $300) 2020
1960 (MS60, $138)
1960 45%, split planchet (MS64, $385) 2020
1960 55% (MS64, $175) 2020
1960-D large date (MS64, $253)
1961 (MS62, $75) (MS64, $63) (MS65, $79)
1961 (AU50, $170) 2020
1961-D (MS63, $73) (MS64, $94) (MS65, $84)
1961-D (MS64, $205) 2020
1962 (MS64, $44)
1962 60% (MS64, $290) 2020
1962-D (MS62, $215) 2020

1963 45% (MS60, $55) (MS62, $130-$216) 2020
1963-D (MS62, $130) (MS63, $200)
1963-D 60% (MS62, $130) 2020
1964 (AU55, $10) (MS61, $28) (MS64, $132)
1964 40% (MS63, $74)
1964 45% (MS60, $115) 2020
1964-D (MS60, $17 - $28) (MS62, $50) (MS63, $57)
1964-D 60% (MS65, $125) 2020
1964-D 90% (MS64, $100) 2020
1965 5% (MS64, $39)
1965 45% (MS67, $999)
1965 65% (MS60, $90) 2020
1966 (AU50, $15) (MS64, $633) (MS66, $550) photo
1966 50% (MS60, $50) 2020
1967 (MS60, $34) (MS62, $47) (MS63, $46-$135) 2020
1967 55% (MS63, $45) 2020
1968 (MS64, $23)
1968 (MS65, $70) 2020
1968-D (AU58, $24) (MS64, $69) (MS65, $87)
1968-D 60% (MS65, $100) 2020
1968-D 15% off center, clipped planchet (MS64, $70)
1968-D off center, curved clip (MS63, $85)
1968-S 10% (MS63, $55) 2020
1968-S 50% (MS67, $460) 2020
1968-S 60% (MS62, $160) 2020
1969-D (AU50, $69) (MS60, $28) (MS63, $37-$50)
(MS64, $21-$92)
1969-x (MS66, $59)
1969 20% (MS65, $104) 2020
1969 60% (MS64, $75) 2020
1969-S 50% (MS66, $375) 2020
1970 15% (MS60, $50) 2020
1970 50% (MS65, $100) 2020
1970 60% (MS60, $55) (MS62, $84) (MS64, $81-$104)
1970-D 45% (MS62, $75) 2020
1970-S large date (MS60, $44-$70) (MS64, $69-$127)

1970-S 45% (NG[25], $70) 2020
1971 60% (MS65, $110) 2020
1971-D (MS63, $42) (MS64, $52)
1971-D 50% (MS60, $45) 2020
1971-S 50% (MS65, $104) (MS66, $150-$253)
1971-S 65% (MS63, $205) 2020
1972 (MS65, $31)
1972-D (MS62, $24) (MS63, $15-$21) (MS64, $27)
1973 50% (MS66, (480) 2020
1973-D (MS64, $26-$863) (MS65, $29-$70) (MS67, $322)
1973-D 50% (MS65, $70) 2020
1973-D 55% (MS60, $435) 2020
1973-S 50% (MS62, $480) 2020
1974 65% (MS60, $50) 2020
1974-D (MS63, $24) (MS60, $45) 2020
1974-D 55% (MS65, $130) 2020
1974-S (MS63, $455) (MS65, $138) 2020
1975 55% (MS64, $105) 2020
1975-D (MS60, $34) (MS64, $39)
1975-D 55% (MS66, $100) 2020
1975-D 60% (MS60, $35) 2020
1976 (MS65, $823-$1,840) 2020
1976 25% (MS65, $825) 2020
1976 50% (MS63, $115) 2020
1976-D (MS65, $34-$188)
1977 65% (MS62, $94) 2020
1977-D (MS63, $25)
1977-D 60% (MS60, $40) 2020
1978 45% (MS63) 2020
1978-D (MS65, $12)
1978-D 60% (MS65, $100) 2020
1979 (MS63, $200) 2020
1979 65% (MS65, $410) 2020
1979-D (MS64, $15)

---

[25] NG-No Grade

1979-D off center on triple curved clip planchet (MS64, $130) 2020
1980 40% (MS63, $65) 2020
1980-D 40% (MS62, $75) 2020
1980-D (AU55, $11) (MS64, $14) (MS65, $59)
1981 (MS60, $23)
1981 35% off center (MS64, $59) 2020
1981 45% off center (MS60, $25) 2020
1981-D 50% off center (MS64, $55) 2020
1981-D (MS63, $42) (MS64, $23)
1981-D off center, clip (MS63, $42) 2018
1982 bronze plated large date (MS63, $35)
1982 bronze plated large date 85% off center (MS64, $120) 2020
1982 bronze plated large date 75% off center (MS63, $70) 2020
1982 bronze plated large date 65% off center (MS66, $120) 2020
1982 bronze plated large date 45% off center (MS60, $40) (MS63, $95) 2020
1982-D bronze plated large date 50% off center (MS62, $100) 2020
1982-D zinc large date (MS65, $35)
1983 (MS60, $10-$30) (MS61, $95) (MS62, $90) (MS65, $30-$35) 2020
1983 60% off center (MS65, $30-$35) 2020
1983 75% off center (MS65, $65) 2020
1983-D 50% off center (MS64, $70) 2020
1984 (MS65, $20)
1984 75% off center (MS63, $28)
1984 50% off center (MS66, $100) 2020
1984-D off center with 3 clips (MS63, $155) 2020
1984-D 50% off center (MS66, $55) 2020
1985 (MS64, $17)
1986 (MS64, $13 - $20)
1986 struck 35% off center (MS66, $135) 2020

1986-D struck 70% off center (MS64, $200) 2020
1987 struck 30% off center (MS65, $45) 2020
1987 struck 45% off center (MS61, $55) 2020
1987-D (MS64, $18)
1988 (MS64, $30-$92)
1988 struck 35% off center (MS64, $60) 2020
1988-D (MS64, $12 - $30)
1988-D struck 50% off center (MS64, $75) 2020
1989 struck 15% off center (MS67, $1,095)
1989 struck 45% off center (MS60, $24-$55) 2020
1989-D (MS65, $23)
1989-D struck 35% off center (MS66, $102) 2020
1989-D struck 65% off center (MS64, $40)
1990 (MS63, $23-$36) (MS64, $30-$40) (MS65, $56)
1990 struck 55% off center (MS66, $70) 2020
1990-D (MS63, $10)
1990-D struck 45% off center (MS62, $70) 2020
1991 (MS62, $26 - $47)
1991 (MS66, $55) 2020
1991-D (MS64, $23)
1991-D struck 70% off center (MS64, $50) 2020
1992 struck 50% off center (MS66, $40) 2020
1992-D struck 65% off center (MS67, $65) 2020
1993 struck 50% off center (MS66, $50) 2020
1993-D (MS64, $19)
1993-D struck 50% off center (MS62, $70) 2020
1994 45% off center (MS65, $100) 2020
1994-D (MS64, $11 - $20)
1994-D 45% off center (MS66, $60) 2020
1995 struck 40% off center (MS66, $90) 2020
1995-D (MS65, $13)
1995-D struck 45% off center (MS65, $65) 2020
1996 (MS64, $30) (MS65, $20-$55)
1996 35% off center (MS64, $60) 2020
1996-D (MS66, $20)
1996-D struck 45% off center (MS60, $30) 2020

1997 (MS60, $34) (MS64, $56-$65) (MS65, $60) 2020
1997-D (MS64, $100) (MS66, $31) 2020
1998 (MS63, $12) (MS65, $18) (MS66, $25-$55)
1998 25% off center (MS64, $75) 2020
1998-D 25% off center (MS62, $35) (MS63, $23-$25)
(MS64, $35) (MS65, $55) (MS66, $31)
1999 (MS63, $10-$70) (MS64, $10-$275) (MS65, $10-$40)
1999-D (MS65, $15) (MS66, $15)
2000 (MS63, $10-$42) (MS64, $40-$805)) (MS65, $16-$45) (MS66, $62) 2020
2000-D Close "AM" struck 20% off center (MS64, $115) 2020
2001 15% off center (MS66, $45) 2020
2002-D struck 60% off center (MS62, $360) 2020
2005 55% off center (MS65, $315) 2020
2007-D 15% off center (MS66, $75) 2020

Chapter Five – Lincoln Cent Planchet Errors

- Clipped Planchets – bow tie, elliptical, fragment, ragged, tapered, thin, and thick planchets
- Cracks, defective, flaws, splits, not sintered, and lamination errors
- Lincoln cents struck on dime planchets
- Unplated planchets
- Wrong metal
- Wrong planchet - struck on foreign planchets

Clips
Bow tie, elliptical, fragment, ragged, tapered, thin, and thick planchets

No date bowtie clip (no grade, $55) (MS64, $490) 2017
No date curved, clipped planchet (MS64, $94) (MS65, $95)
No date defective planchet (MS63, $75) 2017
No date elliptical clip (MS64, $210) 2018
No date fragment (MS60, $212) (MS63, $80) (MS64, $109) (MS66, $165) 2020
No date fragment die cap (MS64, $322) 2020
No date fragment bonded (MS63, $410) 2020
No date fragment double struck (MS64, $150) 2020
No date fragment die cap (MS60, $110) 2020
No date fragment wheat cent (MS63, $138) (MS65, $430) 2020
No date Memorial bowtie clip (MS65, $235-$3,450) 2018
No date Memorial crescent planchet (MS65, $490)
No date Memorial elliptical clip (MS64, $200)
No date Memorial elliptical fragment (MS64, $322) 2020
No date Memorial fragment multiple strike (MS62, $368) 2020

No date Memorial quadruple clipped planchet (MS64, $215)

No date Memorial triple clip (MS66, $155 - $700)
No date ragged clip (MS63, $54) 2017
No date tapered planchet (MS60, $10) (MS64, $16) 2018
No date type II blank planchet (AU55, $13) (MS61, $16)
(MS62, $16-$20) 2018
No date wheat cent elliptical clip (MS64, $230)
No date wheat cent thin planchet, straight clip (MS60, $36)
2018
1917 fragment struck through (MS63, $31) 2020
1929 clipped planchet 6% (AU58, $50) 2018
1936 double clipped (AU58, $36) 2018
1937 fragment strike through (MS63, $518) 2020
1939 fragment strike through (MS65, $36) 2020
1940-S struck on a thin planchet (MS67, $60) 2017
1941 thick planchet (MS64, $165) 2020
1941 thick planchet (brass) (VF20, $345) (AU50, $322)
2020
1942 fragment strike through (AU55, $489) 2020
1942 thick planchet (brass) (VG8, $248) (VF20, $192)
2020
1942 thick planchet (MS62, $1,645) 2020
1943 elliptical clip (AU58, $885) 2020
1944 thick planchet (XF40, $132) (AU55, $440) (MS63,
$276) (MS64, $865-$1,035) 2018
1945 broadstruck, ragged clipped planchet (MS64, $70)
2017
1945 elliptical clip (AU58, $85) (MS64, $90-$140)
1945 thick planchet (MS64, $200-$210)
1945-D clipped planchet (MS66, $93)
1946 elliptical clip (AU58, $220)
1946-S fragment strike through (MS65, $225) 2020
1947-S elliptical clip (MS64, $220)
1948 clipped planchet (VF30, $87)
1951 14% rolled thin planchet (VF25, $29) 2018

1953 tapered planchet (XF40, $26) 2018
1955 tapered planchet (MS62, $1,955) (MS64, $16) 2018
1956 elliptical clip (MS63, $376)
1956 fragment (MS62, $130) 2020
1956 lamination reverse (MS63, $156) 2018
1956 ragged clip (MS65, $90)
1956-D elliptical clip (MS64, $87-$242)
1957-D peeled planchet (MS63, $115) 2020
1959 straight clip planchet (MS64, $50) 2017
1960 curved clip (MS66, $45) 2020
1960 fragment (MS64, $455)
1960 SD fragment (MS64
1961 thin planchet (MS63, $95)
1961-D struck on a 1960-D small date planchet (AU58, $4,600)
1962 ragged clip (MS65, $31)
1962-D fragment (MS64, $1,110) 2020
1964-D 70% crescent clip (MS66, $400) 2020
1964-D bow tie clip (MS63, $633)
1964-D fragment (MS63, $140)
1965 defective planchet (MS65, $105) 2020
1967 thin planchet (MS66. $705)
1969-D fragment (MS60, $52) 2017
1969-S 10% off center, straight clip (MS63, $94)
1971 double clip (MS64, $20) 2020
1971-D thin planchet (MS63, $115)
1971-D thick planchet (MS63, $115) 2020
1972 fragment lamination (MS63, $253) 2020
1972-D thick planchet (MS62, $12) 2018
1976-D thin planchet (MS60, $27) 2018
1977-D 15%/25% off center, three clips (MS64, $153)
1979-D triple curved planchet (MS64, $130)
1980 clip (MS63, $10) 2020
1980-X fragment (MS64, $138) 2020
1981 triple curved planchet (MS64, $130) (MS65, $106) (MS65, $106) 2020

1981 triple curved planchet, broadstruck (MS64, $153) 2020

1981-D double clip (MS63, $25) 2020

1981-D elliptical clip (MS66, $140) 2020

1983 fragment strike through (MS63, $55) 2020

1983-D struck on thin planchet (MS64, $56) 2017

1988 ragged clip (AU58, $185)

1990 elliptical clip (MS65, $75)

1993 thin planchet (MS63, $127)

1998-X curved clipped planchet (MS65, $65) 2017

1999 bow tie clip (MS64, $2,530)

1999 struck on a type I planchet (MS66, $230) 2018

1999 fragment uniface multiple struck (MS64, $403) 2020

1999-X elliptical clip MS66, $118) 2017

Cracks, defective, flaws, lamination, and split planchet errors

1909-S obverse planchet flaw (VF20, $355) 2018

1909-S planchet flaw obverse (MS64, $2,540)

1909-S planchet flaw reverse (VG8, $75-$490) (F12, $65-$647) (VF20, $470-$750) (VF30, $138) (XF40, $750-$820) (MS60, $1,060) 2018

1910-S planchet crack (MS62, $45-$50) 2018

1911-D lamination (XF45, $19) 2019

1914-D planchet flaw (G4, $90-$115) (F12, $160)

1914-D reverse lamination (MS63, $1,955)

1915-D planchet flaw (MS60, $75)

1916 planchet flaw (MS60, $35) 2018

1918-S planchet flaw (AU55, $8) 2018

1919 lamination (VF30, $13) 2019

1920 lamination (MS63, $39) 2019

1921-S lamination (AU50, $34) 2019

1921-S planchet flaw (AU50, $24-$34) 2018

1922 planchet flaw (VF20, $385) 2018

1922-D weak D lamination (AG3, $17.25) 2019

1922-D weak D, planchet flaw (G4, $47) 2018

1927 lamination (XF40, $46-$52) 2018
1927-D planchet flaw (F12, $36) 2018
1927-D lamination, off center 70% (MS60, $48) 2018
1931-S planchet flaw (VF20, $53) 2017
1932-D lamination (MS64, $11) 2018
1934 planchet flaw (MS66, $33) 2018
1941 lamination (XF40, $16) (AU55, $21) 2019
1942-S split planchet (no grade, $70)
1944-D lamination (VF20, $11) 2019
194x split planchet (VF30, $41) (MS63, $36) 2018
1955 defective planchet (MS65, $127)
1955 split planchet (VF30, $32) 2018
1955-D lamination (AU50, $17) 2019
1955-S defective planchet (MS65, $95)
1955-S lamination (AU50, $17) 2019
1956 lamination (MS65, $35) 2019
1956 split planchet (genuine, $36) 2018
1956-D lamination (MS66, $7) 2019
1957-D lamination (XF40, $7) 2019
1958-D lamination (XF45, $24) 2019
1958-D split planchet, off center (AG3, $110)
1959 defective planchet (MS63, $11) (MS64, $48-$135)
2018
1959 defective planchet (MS64, $136)
1959 split planchet (AU50, $41) (no grade, $47) 2018
1960 defective planchet MS64, $19) 2018
1960 LD split planchet (no grade, $51) 2017
1960 SD split planchet (MS60, $50) 2018
1960 split planchet (MS60, $140)
1960-D lamination large date MS63, $41) 2019
1960-D LC split planchet (AU50, $10) 2018
1961 defective planchet (MS64, $140) 2018
1961 split planchet (MS62, $80-$85) (no grade, $65) 2017
1961 split planchet (MS63, $35) 2018
1962-D split planchet, off center (MS63, $155)
1963-D lamination (AU50, $12) 2019

1964 defective planchet (MS62, $36) 2018
1964 sintered planchet (AU58, $32) 2018
1964-D lamination (MS64, $10) 2019
1965 defective planchet (MS65, $85-$110)
1966 lamination (AU53, $12) 2019
1966 split planchet (MS62, $29) 2018
196x split planchet (MS62, $44-$65) 2018
1970-D split planchet (MS60, $29) (MS60, corroded, $29) 2018
1970-D split planchet, detached (MS62, $127-$280) 2018
1982-D occluded gas (MS65, $30) 2020
1987 split planchet (MS63, $128)
1987-D cracked planchet (MS65, $138)
No date Memorial split planchet (no grade, $56) 2017
No date reverse half of a split planchet (MS60, $20) 2018
No date split after strike (MS63, $31) 2018
No date split planchet (MS60, $14) (MS62, $16) 2018
No date split planchet, off center 95% (MS66, $55) 2017
No date zinc type II split planchet (AU50, $24) 2018

Lincoln cents struck on dime planchets
One of the most common planchet errors is the striking of a Lincoln cent on a dime planchet.

A 1996 Lincoln cent on a dime planchet.1925 (VF20, $1,100)
1928 (F12, $1,050)
1941 (XF45, $920)

1941-D (AU58, $1,035)
1942 (VF30, $840) (XF40, $920) (AU58, $2,990-$11,750)
(MS63, $6,200) (MS64, $835)
1943 (VG8, $550) (F12, $1,035) (VF30, $1,530) (VF35,
$1,766-$2,935) (XF40, $466-$5,900) (XF45, $2,650-
$3,450) (AU50, $805-$15,275) (AU53, $2,600) (AU55,
$3,400-$3,900) (AU58, $3,760) (MS60, $4,620) (MS62,
$5,200-$5,590) (MS65, $11,400)
1943-S (AU50, $2,200-$3,525) (AU53, $9,200-$14,100)
(AU55, $8,830) (AU58, $2,100-$4,500) (MS62, $7,800)
2018
1944 (G6, $1,095) (XF40, $3,060-$5,875) (AU50, $865)
(AU53, $3,995-$4,900)
1945-S (XF40, $559) (XF45, $750)
1946-D (XF40, $375) (AU50, $305-$470) 2018
1949 (XF45, $1,495)
1950-D (XF45, $432) 2018
1951 (AU50, $750)
1951-D (MS66, $432) 2018
1951-S (MS62, $2,760)
1952 (AU58, $1,100) (MS63, $2,760) 2018
1952-D (AU58, $3,450)
1952-S (XF45, $1,725) (AU58, $250-$255) 2018
1953 (AU53, $405)
1953-D (AU53, $920) (AU58, $925)
1953-S (XF45, $460)
1954 (AU50, $805)
1955 (AU58, $1,380-$1,725)
1955-S (VF35, $1,960)
1956 (XF40, $325-$575) (AU50, $300-$355) (AU55,
$575-$835) (AU58, $615-$633) (MS60, $1,150) (MS62,
$748-$962) (MS64, $980-$1,155) 2019
1956-D (AU55, $575) (AU58, $564-$2,590) (MS63,
$1,840) (MS64, $1,495) 2019

1957 (VF30, $405-$490) (AU50, $403) (AU55, $450-$647) (AU58, $720-$870) (MS63, $824-$2,300) (MS64, $1,500-$2,300)

1957-D (AU58, $1,150-$2,875) (XF45, $345) (MS62, $1,265) (MS64, $300-$325) 2018

1958 (MS62, $805-$2,469) (MS63, $920)

1958-D (MS63, $1,035)

1959 (XF45, $1,040) (AU50, $225) (AU55, $425) (MS60, $415-$1,060) (MS63, $1,150) (MS64, $1,850-$2,000) 2018

1959-D (AU55, $405) (MS62, $690-$1,020) (MS63, $230-$2,120) (MS64, $1,800-$2,280)[26] 2020

1960 LD (AU50, $575) (AU55, $247-$807) (MS60, $1,380) (MS62, $805-$900) (MS64, $1,500) 2018

1960 SD (AU55, $1,010-$1,300) (MS63, $1,765)

1960 (MS60, $940)

1960-D (AU58, $1,060)

1961 (XF45, $890) (AU55, $460) (MS60, $200-$1,175) (MS62, $990-$1,265) (MS63, $1,710) 2020

1961-D (VF20, $355) (AU50, $805) (MS60, $1,180) 2018

1962 (XF45, $285) (AU50, $582) (AU58, $662-$1,030) (MS62, $822) (MS64, $1,495) 2018

1962-D (AU50, $285-$518) (AU58, $460-$980) (MS62, $840) (MS64, $865) 2020

1963 (AU55, $460) (MS60, $185-$1,530) (MS61, $1,527) (MS62, $807-$4,600) (MS63, $750) 2020

1963-D (AU55, $190-$980) (AU58, $940) (MS65, $1,320)

1964 struck on a clad dime planchet (MS60, $2,500) (MS63, $3,740-$4,850) (MS65, $4,900) 2018

1964 (AU55, $518) (MS60, $375) (MS62, $690-$1,355) (MS63, $1,530-$4,025) (MS64, $2,300-$5,750) (MS65, $385-$4,885) 2018

1964-D (AU50, $489-$547) (AU53, $435) (AU55, $490-$750) (AU58, $690- $945) (MS60, $518) (MS61, $960)

---

[26] One auction for this type coin resulted in a $10,575 bid

(MS62, $242-$1,100) (MS63, $840-$1,265) (MS64, $597-$1,645) (MS65, $7,245) 2020

1965 struck on a clad dime planchet (AU58, $633) (MS60, $345) (MS62, $190-$580) (MS63, $305) (MS64, $405-$633) (MS65, $460-$885) 2020

1965 struck on a silver dime planchet (MS63, $9,200) (MS64, $9,200) (MS65, $1,351-$9,990) 2020

1966 (AU50, $275) (AU55, $323) (MS62, $230-$689) (MS63, $280-$805) (MS64, $275-$1,400) (MS65, $380-$780) (MS66, $345-$410) (MS67, $325) 2018

1967 (F15, $160) (AU55, $190-$200) (AU58, $280-$690) (MS62, $270-$420) (MS63, $300-$460) (MS64, $325-$505) (MS65, $495-$547) (MS66, $432-$547) 2018

1968 (AU58, $190-$220)

1968-D (AU58, $215-$220) (MS60, $185) (MS62, $275-$547) (MS63, $325-$329) (MS64, $495-$1,265) 2018

1968-S (MS63, $690) (MS64, $460-$525) (MS65, $385-$520) 2020

1969 (MS63, $633) (MS64, $405)

1969-D (MS60, $215-$285) (MS63, $465) (MS64, $345) 2018

1969-S (AU55, $375-$562) (MS60, $1,035) (MS61, $455) 2020

1970 (MS64, $365-$430) (MS65, $633-$1,150) 2018

1970-D (AU55, $250-$375) (MS64, $425) 2018

1970-S (MS64, $750-$1,040) (MS65, $520)

1971 (MS62, $200-$330) (MS63, $250-$280) (MS64, $690)

1971-D (AU58, $519) (MS60, $70-$80) (MS62, $329-$750) (MS63, $275-$330) 2020

1971-S (MS64, $805)

1972 (MS63, $250-$255) (MS65, $490) 2018

1972-D (AU58, $300) (MS60, $250-$280) (MS62, $285-$290) (MS64, $375) 2018

1972-S (MS60, $104) (MS66, $622-$1,050)

1973 (AU58, $323) 2018

1973-D (AU55, $205)
1974 (MS64, $250-$300) (MS66, $385) 2018
1974 double denomination (MS63, $1560) 2020
1974-D (AU58, $375) (MS64, $250-$375) 2020
1975 (AU50, $225) (MS60, $305) (MS61, $305) (MS63, $460) 2020
1975-D (MS63, $230-$320) (MS64, $405) 2018
1976 (MS64, $750) (MS65, $250-$300) 2018
1976 25% (MS65, $1,840)
1976-D (MS60, $210-$447) (MS63, $980)
1977 (MS63, $210-$390) (MS64, $370-$420) (MS65, $375) (MS66, $275-$1,210) 2018
1977-D (MS60, $185) (MS63, $275-$280) 2018
1978 (MS60, $200-$432) (MS62, $285-$290) (MS63, 105) (MS64, $250-$1,035) (MS65, $215-$720) (MS66, $485-$605) 2020
1978 (MS60, $150) (MS64, $275-$1,035) (MS65, $240-$405) (MS66, $485) 2020
1978 double denomination on dime (MS65, $720) 2020
1978 obverse strike-through capped die (MS65, $70) 2020
1978 reverse strike-through on dime (MS62, $265) 2020
1978-D 60% (MS65, $100) 2020
1979 (MS60, $200-$210)
1979-D (MS60, $95-$150) (MS65, $575) (MS66, $375) 2020
1980 (MS60, $185) (MS63, $200-$290) 2018
1980 struck on 1980 dime (MS66, $1,100) 2020
1980-D (AU58, $185) (MS62, $240-$315) (MS63, $210-$350) (MS64, $824) 2017
1980-D struck on a silver planchet (MS62, $2,200)
1981 (MS64, $405-$805) (MS65, $520) (MS66, $545) 2020
1981-D (AU58, $210) (MS62, $196-$255) (MS63, $280) (MS65, $196-$345), (MS66, $345) (MS67, $490) 2020

1981-D struck on a 1981 dime planchet (AU58, $205-$230) (MS60, $605) (MS62, $195-$255) (MS63, $275-$870) (MS64, $285-$805) (MS65, $196-$345) 2018
1982 LD (MS63, $185-$518) (MS64, $325-$1,150) (MS65, $575) (MS66, $633-$870) (MS67, $690-$2,300) (no grade, $241)
1982 LD struck on a 1981 dime planchet (MS67, $2,200) 2020
1982[27] (MS63, $530) (MS64, $180) (MS67, $690) 2020
1982 stuck on a clad dime planchet (AU50, $185) (MS63, $370) 2020
1982 LD stuck on a clad dime planchet (AU50, $185) (MS64, $325-$450) (MS65, $242) (MS66, $1,900) 2020
1982 SD (MS64, $185- $435) (MS65, $285-$325) (MS66, $410-$1,265) 2020
1982-D (MS64, $650-$700) 2020
1983 (MS66, $323) 2018
1983 45% off center (MS65, $70) 2020
1983 strike through (MS60, $184) 2020
1984 (MS63, $375-$435) (MS64, $735) (MS66, $490-$1,150) 2020
1985 (MS63, $325) 2018
1986 (MS61, $225-$305) (MS63, $195-$580) (MS64, $460-$860) (MS66, $860-$3,060) 2020
1986 struck on a 1985 dime planchet (MS66, $2,850-$3,060) 2020
1986-D (MS63, $195-$285) 2018
1987 (MS65, $650-$940) (MS66, $250-$840) (MS67, $750-1040[28]) 2020
1987-D (MS64, $1,100) 2020
1988 (MS64, $285-$865) (MS65, $260-$665) (MS66, $520-$1,100) 2020

---

[27] Some PCGS and NGC graded 1982 cents do not specify large or small date.
[28] Stuck on a 1987 dime.

1989 (MS62, $432) (MS63, $920) (MS64, $127-$1,035)
(MS65, $2,115-$2,550) (MS66, $460-$1,380) (MS67,
$750-$1,000) 2020
1990 (MS64, $375-$489) (MS67, $435-$1,380) 2018
1990 (MS67, $750)
1991 (MS63, $575) (MS65, $210-$375) (MS66, $805)
1992 (MS63, $375) (MS65, $750) (MS66, $541) 2018
1993 MS65, $173-$230) (MS67, $633) 2018
1994 (MS63, $575) (MS64, $195-$210) (MS65, $547)
(MS66, $705)
1995 (MS64, $325-$475) (MS65, $375) 2018
1996 (MS63, $375) (MS64, $190-$980) (MS65, $220-$490)
(MS67, $215-$350)
1996 struck on a 1995-D dime (MS65, $2,760)
1996 struck on a 1996 dime (Ms67, $4,100) 2020
1997 (AU55, $127) (MS64, $220-$300) (MS65, $345)
2018
1997 (VF20, $130) (MS62, $280) (MS63, $280-$290)
(MS64, $432) (MS65, $220)
1998 (MS62, $345) (MS63, $385) (MS64, $185-$490)
(MS65, $345-$870) (MS66, $250-$925) (MS67, $822)
2018
1998-D (MS64, $220) (MS65, $489)
1999 (MS62, $230-$333) (MS64, $320-$647) (MS65,
$300-$720) (MS66, $375-$870) 2018
1999 (MS66, $250-$255) (MS67, $925)
1999-D (MS64, $405-$547) (MS65, $200-$253) (MS66,
$770) (MS67, $1,960) 2018
2000 (MS63, $300) (MS64, $230-$285) (MS65, $575-$630)
(MS66, $355-$780) (MS67, $655-$925) (MS68, $930)
2020
2000 with double denomination (MS66, $1,140) 2020
2000-D (MS63, $230-$235) 2018
2001 (MS64, $489) (MS65, $345-$865) (MS66, $345-$635)
(MS67, $720) (MS68, $1,840) 2018
2002-S (PR66, $6,620)

No date (MS62, $559 - $750)

Unplated Planchet Striking
Zinc planchets
1982-D SD (MS62, $95-$100) 2020
1982-D (MS62, $60) (MS63, $55-$60) 2020
1983 (AU50, $85) (MS64, $60-$245) (MS65, $100) (MS66, $285) 2020
1984-D (MS63, $65)
1986-D (MS63, $286) (MS64, $105) (MS60, $69) 2020
1987-D (MS63, $80) 2020
1988-D (MS63, $185) (MS64, $375) (MS65, $662)
1989-D (MS64, $60-$70) 2020
1988 (MS63, $55) 2020
1990 (MS63, $127) (MS64, $185-$190) (MS65, $155) (MS66, $705) 2020
1996 (MS64, $115)[29]

Wrong Metal
1915 struck on incorrect metal planchet (XF45, $1,615)
1921-S bow y planchet (MS63, $450-$1,495)
1921-S silver scrap planchet (MS63, $1,495) 2020
1940 struck on a brass planchet (XF40, $88-$150) (XF45, $95-$110)
1941 struck on a brass planchet (VF20, $345) (XF40, $80-$305) (XF45, $127-$340) (MS63, $94-$355) 2018
1941 struck on a thick brass planchet (VF20, $205) (VF35, $128) (XF40, $127) (XF45, $350) (AU55, $325) (MS63, $405)
1941 struck on incorrect metal (VF35, $200) (AU58, $3,060) (MS65, $633)
1942 struck on a thick brass planchet (VF35, $325) (XF40, $127) (MS62, $1,645)

---

[29]

1942 struck on incorrect metal composition (VF20, $560) (AU50, $990)

1943 struck on a bronze planchet (AU50, $46,000) (AU58, $218,500-$305,500) (MS61, $180,000) (MS62, $282,000) (no grade, $88,200)

1943 struck on a steel blank planchet (no grade, $190-$220)

1943 struck on an experimental planchet (AU55, $58,750) (MS63, $12,000) 2020 2018

1943-S struck on a bronze planchet (VF35, $141,000-$207,000) (AU53, $216,000-$228,000) (AU55, $212,000) (AU58, $252,000-$282,000) 2018

1944 struck on a brass planchet (MS63, $425-$1,295) 2017

1944 struck on a zinc coated steel planchet (XF40, $6,325-$7,100) (AU50, $5,875-$33,600) (AU55, $11,500-$26,400) (AU58, $30,500-$34,500) 2018

1944-D struck on a zinc coated steel planchet (VF30, $4,150-$28,750) (VF35, $7,700) (AU50, $10,350-$60,375) (AU53, $32,500-$37,375) (AU55, $60,375) (MS62, $54,000-$92,000) (MS63, $79,300-$115,000) (MS65, $4,400) 2018

1944-S struck on a zinc planchet (MS66, $373,750)

1958-D scrap planchet (MS64, $180) 2020

1959 struck on a brass planchet (MS65, $1,900) 2017

1962 scrap planchet (MS63, $450) 2020

1971-S struck on an aluminum planchet (AU58, $8,100)

1980-D scrap planchet (MS65, $175) 2020

1982 double struck on 84% silver, 16% copper planchet (MS64, $1,150) 2020[30]

1982 LD scrap planchet (MS60, $185) 2020

1982-D SD struck on zinc, no copper plating (MS61, $44) (MS62, $44-$95) (MS65, $323) 2018

---

[30] Posted in double struck listing also.

1983 struck on a copper planchet (AU55, $16,450) (MS62, $23,500) (MS63, $18,900) 2020

1983 transitional error wrong planchet (genuine, $1,880) 2018

1983 zinc planchet with some copper (MS64, $127) (MS65, $36) 2020

1983 zinc, no copper plating (AU50, $85-$90) (MS60, $42-$75) (MS64, $95-$127) (MS65, $40-$100) 2018

1983-D struck on bronze planchet (AU55, $17,500) 2018

1984-D partial plating (MS60, $45) 2020

1985-D zinc, no copper plating (MS60, $80) (MS62, $65-$70) (MS63, $33-$70) (MS64, $215) (MS65, $75-$85) (MS66, $285) 2018

1986-D zinc, no copper plating (MS63, $107) (MS64, $105-$150) (MS66, $180-$190)

1987-D zinc, no copper plating (MS60, $38) 2018

1989-D struck on a wheat cent type planchet (MS65, $7,500)

1989-D struck on a zinc, no copper plating planchet (MS64, $70) (MS65, $65-$85) 2018

1990-D struck on a copper planchet 3.1 grams (MS64, $5,650)

1993 struck on zinc, no copper plating (MS63, $110)

1994-D zinc, no copper plating (MS65, $60) 2019

1995-D zinc, no copper plating (MS62, $56) (MS63, $80-$85) (MS64, $100) 2017

1996-D zinc, no copper plating (MS64, $130) (MS65, $127)

1998 zinc, no copper plating (MS64, $127)

1998 zinc, no copper plating (MS65, $275)

1998 struck on bronze/clad/steel planchet (MS66, $920)

2000 partial copper planchet (MS63, $95)

2000-D zinc, no copper plating (MS62, $145)

No date Memorial zinc alloy (MS64, $288) (MS66, $865)

No date steel cent blank (MS62, $65-$210) 2017

Wrong Planchet - Foreign Planchets

Lincoln cents struck on foreign planchets

1919 foreign planchet (XF40, $250-$255) 2018
1919 Argentina planchet (AU55, $345) 2018
1920 Columbia planchet (VF25, $460) 2018
1920 Cuba planchet (MS64, $2,875)
1920 foreign planchet (AU50, $1,060)
1920 Argentina planchet (F12, $330) 2018
1940 foreign planchet (MS62, $805)
1941 Netherlands planchet (AU50, $1,620)
1941 Panama planchet (MS65, $3,745-$4,995)
1942 Netherlands 25 cent planchet (VG10, $65)
1942 Ecuador planchet (VF35, $1,900) (XF40, $1,415)
1943 Cuba planchet (MS62, $4,995-$38,189)
1943 Curacao planchet (F12, $7,475) (XF40, $7,650-$14,950)
1943 Netherlands planchet (MS62, $24,000)
1943-D Australia planchet (AU50, $4,320)
1943-D struck on Peru planchet (XF40, $6,450)
1944 Netherlands planchet (MS63, $5,180-$7,650)
1944 Philippines planchet (MS62, $5,175-$6,470)
1945 Netherlands planchet (AU58, $2,530) (MS64, $345-$1,420) (MS65, $432) 2018
1945 Ethiopia planchet (MS62, $1,095-$1,645) (MS65, $564)
1953 Cuba planchet (MS62, $3,055)
1955 Venezuela planchet (MS60, $1,612)
1956 Honduras planchet (MS64, $2,100)
1957 Honduras planchet (MS66, $647)
1958 Cuba planchet (AU50, $489) (AU58, $1,525) (MS63, $1,120-$3,525) (MS64, $920) (MS65, $1,530) 2015
1958 Cuba planchet, 1958 Lincoln cent (MS63, $3.535) 2020
1958 Cuba planchet, overstruck (MS65, $4,935) 2020
1959 Dominican Republic (MS63, $2,820) 2020
1959 Philippine 10 cent planchet (MS64, $660) 2020
1962 Philippine 10 cent planchet (MS65, $575) 2018

1968 Canadian planchet (MS62, $405) (MS64, $1,420) 2018

1969 Canadian planchet (MS64, $345) 2018

1969 Canadian planchet, double struck (MS62, $2,760) 2018

1969-S Canadian planchet, double struck (MS62, $3,820) 2020

1972-D Philippine planchet ($200-$210)

1979 foreign planchet (MS64, $85)

1980 Dominican Republic planchet (MS62, $345) (MS64, $345) 2018

1982 LD struck on Dominican Republic planchet (MS64, $690) 2020

1995 foreign planchet (MS62, $110)

1996 foreign planchet (MS64, $196)

1996 Singapore planchet (MS63, $90-$270)

1997-D foreign planchet (MS64, $230-$235) 2018

1998 foreign planchet (MS63, $115-$128) (MS67, $95-$432) (MS68, $127-$288) 2020

2000 foreign planchet (MS67, $290) 2020

2000-D foreign planchet (MS64, $115)

No date Memorial type II ten cent planchet (MS64, $1,555) (MS65, $1,555)

Chapter Six – Lincoln Cent Mint Striking Errors

- "BIE" errors and filled numbers
- Bonded pair
- Broadstruck
- Brockage
- Counter brockage
- Die adjustment strike
- Die cap
- Die clash
- Double struck
- Fold over strike/ Fold overstrike
- Indent
- Mated pair
- Mules
- Multiple struck
- Off center
- Oddities
- Partial collar
- Rotated die
- Saddle struck
- Strike-through
- Uniface strike

Coins are listed by date first followed by all error notations. The 1982 Lincoln cents were not always noted as large (LD) and small date (SD) on encapsulated holders.

Wheat cent no date
No date brockage (AU58, $82) (MS63, $80)
No date broadstruck brockage (PR61, $70)
No date broadstruck indent (MS64, $58)
No date counter brockage (MS63, $138) (MS64, $40) 2020
No date die adjustment strike (NG, $155-$235) 2020

No date die adjustment strike (AU50, $230) (MS60, $70) 2020
No date fold over strike (MS62, $230) 2018
No date saddle strike (MS63, $29-$33) 2018
No date struck on dime (MS63, $33) (MS64, $115)

No date Memorial Cents
No date fold over strike, zinc (MS64, $750) 2020
No date multiple struck (MS64, $100) 2020
No date brockage (MS60, $20 - $35) (MS63, $25) (MS64, $15 - $25) (MS65, $22-$70) 2017
No date broadstruck brockage (MS64, $41) (MS65, $49-$60) 2018
No date capped die wheat (MS63, $25) 2018
No date broadstruck brockage (MS64, $26 - $80) (MS65, $7)
No date brockage (MS63, $30)
No date brockage die cap (MS64, $75)
No date brockage Indent (MS64, $115)
No date brockage strike-through (MS66, $30 - $40)
No date capped die (MS64, $17) 2018
No date double struck (AU55, $33) (MS64, $45 - $115) (MS65, $30 - $380)
No date double struck saddle struck (MS64, $70) (MS65, $139) (MS66, $49)
No date double struck split planchet (MS64, $49) 2018
No date fold over strike (MS62, $230 - $460) (MS63, $1,840) (MS64, $633)
No date fold over strike (MS63, $1,840) (MS64, $650 - $755)
No date saddle struck (MS62, $212) (MS63, $33) (MS64, $65 - $94) (MS65, $165) (MS66, $445) 2018
No date triple struck (MS64, $300) (MS65, $405) (MS66, $155)
No date triple struck on silver dime (MS64, $2,600) (MS66, $650) (MS67, $7,700)

No date uniface off center (MS65, $22) 2020
196x counter brockage (MS64, $255) 2020
197x counter brockage (MS63, $92-$170) 2020
1909 obverse strike-through capped die (MS63, $65) 2018
1909 VDB double struck rotated collar (MS60, $153) 2018
1909 VDB obverse strike-through (AU details, $10) 2018
1910 double struck 15% off center (AU58, $405 - $805)
1910 uniface struck (AU58, $4,325-$6,900) 2020
1911 double struck (XF45, $258)
1912 double struck 10% off center (AU53, $435)
1916 broadstruck (MS63, $104 -$299)
1916-D broadstruck (MS64, $575)
1916-S broadstruck (MS63, $145)
1917 broadstruck (MS63, $184)
1918 broadstruck type 1 planchet (MS64, $115-$165)
1918 double struck 55% off center (MS65, $1,725)
1918 double struck 85% off center (AU58, $748)
1918 multiple struck nine times (F15, $2,100)
1919 broadstruck (MS64, $299) (MS65, $432)
1920 broadstruck (AU55, $71)
1920 broadstruck on an Argentina planchet (MS62, $690)
1920 broadstruck straight clip (MS63, $330) 2018
1920 brockage 40% off center (VG10, $633)
1922 strike trough (VF25, $664)
1923 partial collar multi struck close overlap (MS62, $312)
2020
1936 broadstruck (MS62, $690) (MS65, $87)
1937 broadstruck split planchet (MS63, $51) 2017
1939 strike through fragment (MS65, $25) 2018
1941 broadstruck (MS60, $127)
1941 broadstruck clip (MS60, $127)
1941 double struck 15% off center (MS64, $412)
1943 die adjustment strike (NG, $402-$432) 2020
1943 double struck 80% off center (MS64, $1,763)
1943 double struck 90% off center (MS61, $604)
1942 uniface struck (XF45, $1060) 2020

1944 double struck 10% off center (MS63, $588)
1944-S double struck 60% off center (MS60, $329)
1945 broadstruck (MS63, $92) (MS65, $31)
1949 double struck 80% off center (MS64, $150)
1952-D double struck (MS63, $1,116)
1952-S double struck (MS63, $374)
1954-D double struck (VF35, $230)
1954-S broadstruck (MS64, $99)
1955 double struck 70% off center (MS64, $330)
1955-D double struck 80% off center (MS64, $212)
1955-D strike-through (MS66, $310) 2020
1957 double struck rotated collar (AU53, $240) 2020
1958-D double struck 85% off center (MS63, $184 - $276)
1959 double struck rotated collar (MS62, $580) 2020
1960 triple struck (PR65, $115-$285) (PR67, $145-$190) (PR68, $305) 2020
1960 triple struck large over small date (PR66, $130) (PR67, $215) 2020
1960-D large date double struck fold over, 95% off center (MS62, $87)
1963-D die cap strike-through (MS63, $375) 2020
1964 broadstruck brockage (MS65, $81)
1964 brockage (MS64, $140) 2020
1964 die cap (MS64, $255-$505) (MS66, $1,150) 2020
1964 double struck off center (MS63, $285) 2020
1964 double struck 65% off center (MS63, $435) 2020
1964 double struck 75% off center (MS64, $88-$99)
1964 double struck 80% off center (MS64, $74)
1964 multiple strikes (MS65, $1,610)
1964 saddle struck (MS60, $32) (MS64, $76-$180)
1964 triple struck (MS63, $440) (MS64, $403-$940) (MS65, $550-$1,150) 2020
1964 triple struck off center (MS65, $825) 2020
1964 triple struck saddle struck (MS64, $805)
1964-D broadstruck clipped planchet (MS65, $87)
1964-D die adjustment strike (NG, $94) (MS62, $51) 2020

1964-D double struck fold over(MS63, $235) 2020
1964-D double struck (MS60, $44)
1964-D double struck 90% off center (MS60, $44)
1965 broadstruck indented (MS64, $39) 2018
1965 broadstruck wheel mark (MS60, $25-$40) 2020
1965 brockage (MS63, $25)
1965 die cap (MS63, $285) 2020
1965 double struck 60% off center (MS64, $173 - $179)
1965 double struck 70% off center (MS60, $69)
1965 double struck 75% off center (MS65, $200) (MS66, $318) 2016
1965 quadruple struck (MS63, $330) 2016
1965 triple struck (MS64, $1,610)
1967 double struck 95% off center uniface (MS60, $47)
1968-S double struck (PR65, $4,340) 2020
1968-S double struck 50% off center (MS64, $376) 2015
1968-S strike through capped die (MS63, $26) 2018
1969-D double struck (MS62, $63) (MS64, $1,235) 2020
1969-D triple struck saddle struck (MS65, $587)
1969-S strike-through obverse. (PR65, $1,175) 2020
1970-D double struck (MS63, $207) 2020
1970-D double struck 45% off center (MS62, $84) 2020
1970-D double struck 75% off center (MS64, $104) 2020
1970-D double struck 85% off center (MS60, $55) 2020
1970-D fold over triple saddle strike (MS62, $1,322) 2020
1970-D saddle struck (MS66, $550) 2020
1970-S strike-through obverse (MS64, $55) 2020
1970-S triple struck (PR65, $80-$110) (PR66, $200) (PR67, $470) 2020
1970-S triple struck 35% off center (MS64, $1,035[1]) (MS64, $375) 2020
1971 indent partial collar (MS65, $44) 2020
1971-D brockage reverse (MS64, $2,280) 2020
1971-D capped die strike-through (MS65, $85) 2020
1971-D double (MS62, $863)
1971-D double struck 75% off center (MS60, $36)

1971-D double struck 85% off center (MS60, $102)
1971-D double struck 95% off center (MS62, $865)
1971-D strike-through (NG[31], $35) 2020
1971-D triple struck 70% off center (MS62, $259)
1971-D uniface double strike off center (MS60, $102) 2020
1972-D double struck fold over (MS63, $306-$402)
1972-D double struck fold over uniface (MS63, $305) 2020
1972-D fold overstrike (MS60, $575)
1972-S bonded pair (MS63, $3,738) 2020
1973 die cap strike-through (MS64, $140) (MS65, $90) 2020
1973 saddle struck (MS64, $305) 2020
1973 triple struck 80%/95% off center (MS64, $259)
1973-D two planchets struck together (MS62, $100) 2020
1973-S double struck (PR67, $978)
1973-S double stuck fold over(MS64, $865)
1974 double struck 55% off center (MS65, $130)
1974 double struck 60% off center (MS60, $118)
1974 indent partial collar (MS64, $85) 2020
1974-D brockage partial collar (MS63, $305) 2020
1975-D die cap (MS65, $360) 2020
1975-D double struck, broadstruck (MS65, $170) 2020
1975-D mated pair (MS66, $375) 2018
1975-D strike-through die cap (MS64, $15) 2011
1976 die break obverse (MS65, $110) 2020
1976 double struck (MS64, $80) 2020
1977 double struck (MS63, $360) 2020
1977-D broadstruck 40% straight clip (MS66, $150) 2020
1977-D broadstruck triple curved planchet (MS61, $80) 2020
1978-D brockage 40% (MS62, $125) 2020
1978-D die break (MS64, $60) 2020
1978-D double struck 65% off center (MS63, $138) 2011
1979 die cap (MS64, $330) 2020

---

[31] No Grade

1979 double struck 65% off center (MS63, $80) 2020
1979-D broadstruck (MS60, $20) 2020
1979-D double struck on split planchet (NG[32], $520) 2020
1979-D saddle struck (MS64, $305) 2020
1980 double struck (MS65, $52)
1980 double struck fold over(MS65, $185) 2020
1980 double struck 85% off center (MS65, $183 - $188)
1980-D broadstruck (MS63, $26) 2020
1980-D triple struck (MS62, $345)
1980-D strike through grease (AU50, $25) 2020
1981 bonded pair (MS64, $1,762) 2020
1981 double struck fold over(MS64, $125)
1981 triple struck 50%/70% (MS64, $1,035)
1981-D mated pair (MS63, $255) 2020
1981-D triple curved clip (MS64, $152)
1982 broadstruck brockage (MS65, $80)
1982 broadstruck out of collar (MS64, $44-$800) 2020
1982 LD broadstruck (AU55, $70) 2020
1982 brockage and partial collar (MS63, $155) 2020
1982 bronze triple struck saddle struck (MS65, $235)
1982 capped die strike through (MS64, $40) 2020
1982 double struck on 84% silver 16% copper planchet
(MS64, $1,150) 2020
1982 SD double struck rotated collar (MS66, $160) 2020
1982 indent 35% (MS63, $80-$90) 2020
1982 mated pair (MS66,1,035) 2020
1982 strike-through 40% of obverse (MS63, $50) 2020
1982 LD unplated double struck (MS64, $100) (MS65, $70)
1983 broadstruck (MS63, $28)
1983 brockage (MS60, $22)
1983 die break (MS64, $20) 2020
1983 double struck 75% off center (MS60, $40) (MS64,
$376)
1984 broadstruck and multiple struck (MS65, $130) 2020

---

[32] NG – Not graded but encapsulated

1984 obverse die break (MS64, $15-$75) (MS65, $30) 2020

1984 reverse die break (MS64, $175) 2020

1984 double struck (MS67, $3,290) 2020

1984-D double struck 85% off center (MS64, $141)

1985 bonded pair (MS68, $885)

1985 bonded obverse die cap (MS62, $633)

1985 double struck (AU50, $28)

1985 double struck 70% off center (MS64, $65)

1985 double struck 75% off center (MS64, $75-$95) 2020

1985 struck on a dime planchet (MS62, $405) 2018

1986 major die break widespread (MS62, $25) 2020

1987 major die break widespread (MS65, $35-$70) 2020

1987 double struck (MS63, $115) (MS64, $30) 2020

1987 double struck 75% off center (MS63, $115) (MS64, $74)

1987 fold over strike (MS63, $633)

1987-D obverse and reverse struck though (no grade, $25) 20203, $173) 2020

1987-D triple struck (MS6

1988 broadstruck brockage (MS63, $24)

1988 double struck fold over(MS63, $110-$300) (MS65, $147)

1988-D double struck flipover (MS60, $45) 2020

1989 broadstruck (MS63, $10) 2020

1989 broadstruck brockage (AU55, $14) (MS63, $70) 2020

1989 centered broadstruck (XF40, $300) 2020

1989 double struck 65% (MS66, $70)

1989 double struck indent (MS64, $145) 2020

1989 fold over strike (MS65, $960) (MS66, $840-$1,250) 2020

1990 double struck (MS62, $110) 2020

1990 double struck broad struck (MS64, $155) 2020

1991-D double struck 70% (MS63, $79)

1992 double struck 75% (MS60, $34) (MS63, $67)

1992 obverse die cap brockage (MS62, $121)

1993 double struck (MS65, $58)
1993 double struck 80% off center (MS60, $58)
1993 double struck broadstruck stretch strike (MS64, $18)
2018
1993 double struck brockage (MS60, $24) (MS63, $22 -
$44) (MS64, $19 - $56) (MS65, $40)
1994 broadstruck brockage (MS63, $18)
1994 double struck 70% off center (MS62, $184)
1995 broadstruck (MS63, $59) 2017
1995 counter brockage (MS63, $18) 2018
1995 die cap (MS63, $52) 2018
1995 double struck (MS64, $10) (MS65, $40)
1995 double struck 70% off center (MS65, $97)
1995 double struck 75% off center (MS60, $85)
1995 double struck counter brockage, fold over(MS63, $18)
1995 triple stuck 75%/85% off center (MS64, $165)
1996 die cap (MS63, $115) (MS64, $490)
1996 double struck 25% off center (MS66, $400)
1996 double struck 65% - 80% off center (MS61, $74 - $95)
(MS65, $55)
1996 double struck brockage 45% off center (MS64, $200)
1996 triple struck (MS68, $550)
1996-D triple struck 75% off center (MS62, $120 - $155)
1997 counter brockage (MS64, $11) 2020
1997 die cap (MS68, $1,265)
1997 double struck 15% (MS68, $260)
1997 double struck 75% (MS65, $60)
1997 double struck broadstruck (MS66, $51 - $375)
1997 reverse die cap (MS66, $460)
1998 bonded pair (MS66, $765-$1,310) (MS66, $1,725)
1998 broadstruck brockage (MS61, $35) (MS64, $35 - $82)
(MS65, $31)
1998 broadstruck counter brockage (PR65, $60) 2017
1998 brockage (MS65, $31)
1998 counter brockage (MS64, $13) 2020
1998 counter brockage die cap (MS66, $80) 2020

1998 die cap (MS65, $230) (MS66, $300-$410) 2018
1998 die cap bonded pair (three pieces) (MS63, $3,450)
1998 double struck (MS65, $70-$80)
1998 double struck broadstruck (MS66, $105)
1998 mated pair (MS64, $1,150) (MS65, $2,070)
1998 multiple strike (MS65, $70-$490) 2018
1998 obverse die cap (MS66, $432-$750)
1998 obverse die cap (MS67, $647)
1998 reverse die cap (MS65, $85) (MS66, $115-$375)
1998 reverse die cap (MS66, $127)
1998 struck on a dime planchet (MS66, $375) 2018
1998 double struck on 1997 (MS65, $2,160) 2020
1998-D die cap (MS66, $60) 2017
1998-S double struck rotated collar (PR69, $5,700) 2019
1999 broadstruck (MS65, $185) 2018
1999 broadstruck (MS66, $60-$65) 2018
1999 broadstruck counter brockage (MS66, $54-$82) 2020
1999 broadstruck indent (MS64, $52) 2018
1999 broadstruck partial brockage (MS64, $22) 2018
1999 die cap bonded pair (MS64, $1,840) (MS64, $2,070)
1999 double struck (MS64, $65) (MS66, $87) 2017
1999 double struck indent (MS63, $49) (MS66, $115) 2018
1999 fold over (MS66, $60-$70) 2017
1999 mated pair (MS66, $190)
1999 multiple strikes (MS65, $895)
1999 multiple strikes bonded pair (MS65, $2,100)
1999 obverse die cap (PR62, $80) (MS65, $765)
1999 obverse die cap bonded, double struck (MS64, $605)
1999 reverse die break (MS66, $140)
1999 reverse die cap (MS63, $52) (MS64, $52) (MS65,
$46-$65) 2018
1999-D obverse die cap (MS64, $575)
1999-D double struck off center uniface (MS67, $59) 2020
2000 brockage broadstruck (MS64, $35) 2018
2000 double struck (MS60, $28) 2018
2000 triple struck (MS65, $120) 2020

2000 fold over strike (MS62, $95)
2000 mated pair (MS64, $300) 2018
2000 obverse die cap (MS67, $415)
2000-D double struck (MS64, $275) (MS65, $360[33]) 2020
2000-D mated pair (MS65, $330) 2018
2001 counter brockage (MS65, $30) 2020
2001 double struck (MS62, $58) (MS64, $49) 2018
2001 mated pair (MS64, $300) 2018
2001-D obverse die cap (MS66, $489) 2018
2001-X fold overstrike (MS63, $300) 2018
2002-D close "AM" struck 20% off center (MS64, $115)

---

[33] This coin was also off center with the second strike.

Chapter Seven – Photographs of Errors

This chapter contains listings with photographs of the most obvious doubled die errors. There is no valid reason why some D over D or D over S issues command such a wide range of bids at auction. Values do not attribute to the number of coins certified, nor the grade of the coins.

1909 VDB DDO doubling on 190 and RTY

1909-S S over S

1910-S S over S

1911-D D over D PCGS XF45

1911-D Triple D

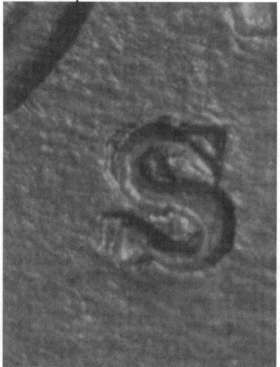

1911-S S over S

1917 doubled die. The doubling of all letters and numbers

1922 no D Lincoln cent.
There are examples of this error in all grades. Many error coins, such as this coin missing the D, were not recognized as mint errors until the first coin guides printed in the 1940s revealed the issue.

1925-S S over S

1927 DDO

1928-S Large S over S

1929-S S over S

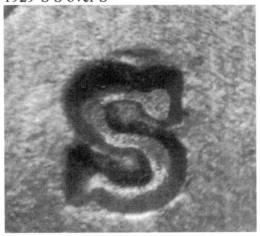

1930-S S over S

1934 DDO – partial numbers below the date

1934-D D over D

1935 DDO

1936 DDO 2 Doubling is primarily on the date

1936 DDO 3 Doubling on LIBERTY – no date doubling

1936 DDR

1936-D Doubled Die

1937 DDR – E. PLURIBUS UNUM – Strongest on the "R"
Note: There are many versions.

There are four variations of this doubled die coin with degrees of doubling. DDO type one contained doubling in the date, LIBERTY, and the motto and considered the strongest showing in the photographs above. DDO type two shows doubling in the date. DDO 3 shows doubling in the motto and the date, but it is not very pronounced.

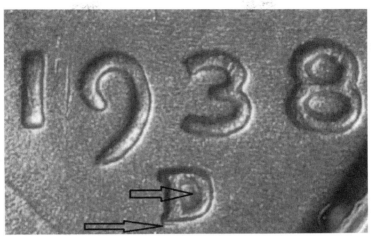

1938-D D over D

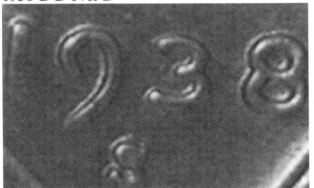

1938-S S over S

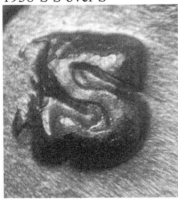

1938-S Triple S

1939 DDO prominent doubling of Liberty

1939-S S over S

1940-D D over D

1940-S S over S

1941 DDO

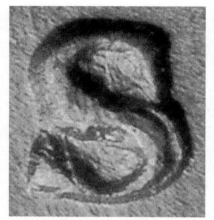

1941-S S over large S

1941-S S over S

1942-D D over D

1942-S S over S

1942-S Triple S

1943 Doubled Die

1943-D DDO

1943-S S over S

1944-D DDO Doubling on the date

1944-D D over D

1944-D D over S

1945 DDO Letters doubled "IN GOD WE TRUST"

1945-S S over S

1945-S Doubled Liberty

1946-D D over D

1946-S S over D

1946-S DDO

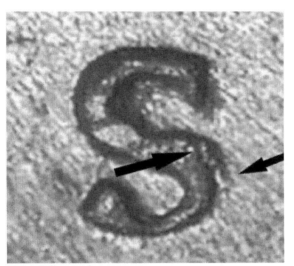

1946-S S over S

1947 Doubled Die

1947-S S over S

1948-S S over S

1949-D D over D

1949-S DDO "4"

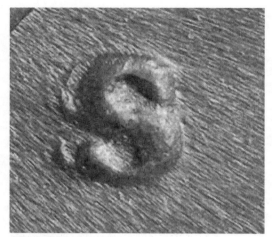

1949-S S over S

1950-D D over Horizontal D

1950-S Normal "S"

1950-S S over S

1951-D DDO

1951-D D over D

1951-D D over S

1952-D D over S

1952-S S over S

1952-D D over D

1953-D D over D

1953-S S over S

1954-D D over D

1954-D D/D/D

1954-S S over S

One of the most sought-after doubled die cents is 1955.

1955 DDO

1955-D DDO

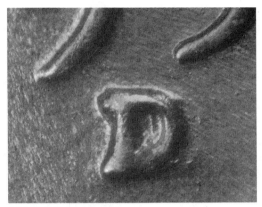

1955-D D over D

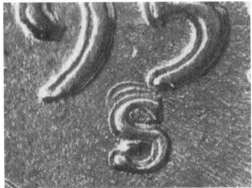

1955-S S/S/S

1956-D D over D

1957-D DDO filled lower B (author owned)

1957- D D over D

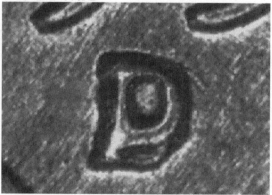

1957-D D/D/D

1958 DDO

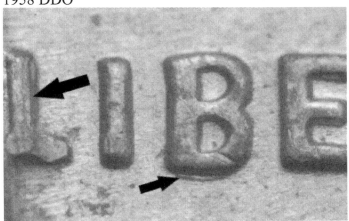

1958-D DDO

1959 DDO

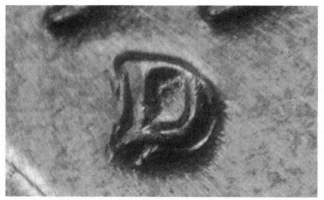

1959-D D/D/D

1960-D D over D large date

1960-D D over D large over small

1960 small date over large.

1961 DDO – some varieties are less pronounced.

1961-D D over horizontal D

1962 DDO

1963-D DDO

1964 DDO "LIBERTY"

1964 DDR

1968-S DDR

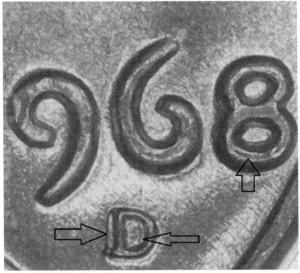

1968-D D over D

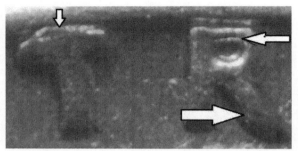

1968-S DDO Doubling occurs "IN GOD WE TRUST"

1969-S doubled die

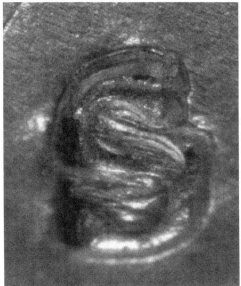

1970-S S over S RPM large date

1971 DDO

1971-S DDO Liberty

1971-S DDO

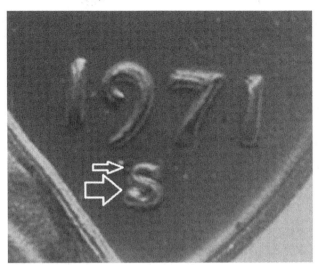

1971-S S over S

1972 DDO (see photograph for the date below)

1972 Doubled date

1980 doubled die "LIBERTY"

1981-S Filled S

1982 DDO large date

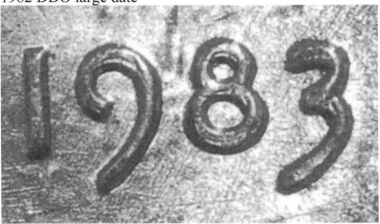

1983 DDO

1983 DDR – Doubling in the One and Cent

1984 doubled ear

1984 DDO

1985-D D over D

1992-D close AM and normal AM

1994 DDR

1995 DDO

1995-D DDO Doubling in all letters and mint mark

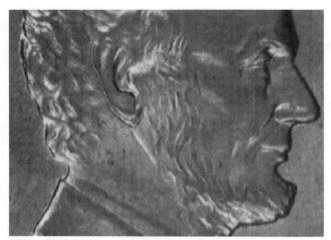

1997 doubled ear Lincoln cent

1998-S DDO and rotated

6

DDO doubling of the date and lettering

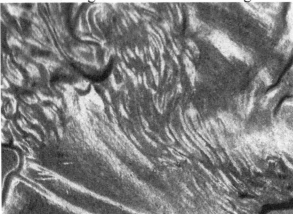

2006 doubled ear

2009 Formative Years cent with doubling of fingers

2013 DDO

2015 DDO

Doubled Die versus Mechanical Doubling

Collectors need to be careful when purchasing what appears to be a doubled die or RPM coin from unprofessional sources, including eBay. Doubled die coins have raised letters, dates, or mintmarks like the intended strike.

The doubling of GO is clearly apparent

Above is a Lincoln cent with mechanical doubling.

*C*hapter Eight– Variations

Variations are not errors, but an intentional change made by the US Mint. In the early days of minting coins, the mint made many die changes for the same coin year and denomination. As the minting process became more refined, fewer changes were necessary.

Today, variations are the result of creating more than one hub slightly different from each other. The most famous Lincoln cent variation is the 1909-S VDB. The mint intentionally removed the large VDB on the reverse of the coin during the 1909 mintage.

Subsequently, the 1960 Lincoln cent production resulted in a small and large date from the Philadelphia and Denver mints.

Comparison of the 1960 small date to left and large date to the right.

The small and large date 1970-S coins above is recognized by the 7 to the tops of the 1, 9, and 0.

Below is an overlay of the 1974 large and small dated Lincoln cents.

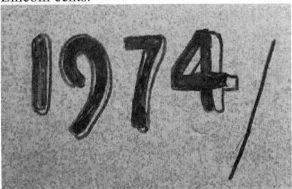

1974 small and large date overlay

In 1974, the US Mint adjusted the 1974 date, moving it further away from the rim. The curved line in the photograph represents the rim. The large dated 1974 is in black, further away from the rim. The small date is outlined with no color. Part of the one, nine, and seven are slightly different. The position of the four on the date is significantly changed.

1982 large and small dated Lincoln cents

In 1982, the mint issued seven different Lincoln cents. The seven cents included large and small dates and zinc and copper cents. The dates on the coins are visibly different from large to small dates. The zinc/copper plated coins weigh 2.54 grams versus 3.11 grams for copper coins.

Only recognized in this guide is a variation of the three in 1983 dated coins. The "spoon" three is wider on the bottom of the three. Since two BU coins were used for validation, the difference is recognized as authentic.

1983 spoon three

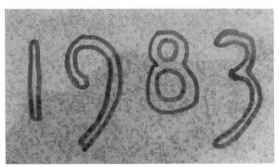

1983 with a standard three

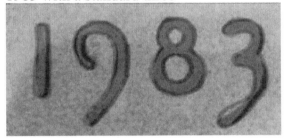

1983 Lincoln cent overlaid

1985 overlaid with two "die set" mintages of the 1985-D

In the 1980s, The Philadelphia mint made all the mint dies for distribution without mintmarks. The Denver and San

Francisco mints added at the mintmark to the dies. The preparation of new dies in Denver resulted in different "D" placements. Some of the "D" mintmarks tilt to the right or the left for the same dated coins.

Chapter Nine – History of the Lincoln Cent and Design Changes

History of the Lincoln Cent

The Lincoln one-coin coin was issued in 1909. The style of the coin was a radical change from previous coin styles. The 1909 Lincoln cent was the first U.S. coin with a portrait of a President.

"The U.S. Mint was uncertain of the public reception placing a President of the United States on a coin. Since it was the 100th anniversary of Abraham Lincoln's birth, the general population was receptive.[34]"

"The only person invited to participate in the formulation of the new design was Victor David Brenner. President Theodore Roosevelt was so impressed with this outstanding sculptor's talents that the President singled out Brenner for the commission. President Lincoln's likeness on the obverse of the coin is an adaptation of a plaque Brenner executed several years earlier, which had come to President Roosevelt's attention.[35]"

"LIBERTY and the date --, the motto In God We Trust appeared for the first time on a coin of this denomination. Of interest is the fact that Congress passed the Act of March 3, 1865, authorizing the use of this motto on our coins during Lincoln's tenure in office.[36]"

A study of three models for the coin's reverse resulted in the approval of a straightforward design bearing two wheat-heads in memorial style. Between these, in the center of the

---

[34] US Mint website
[35] US Mint website
[36] US Mint website

coin, are the denomination and UNITED STATES OF AMERICA, while curving around the upper border is the national motto, E Pluribus Unum means "One out of Many."[37]

"No legislation existed for the new design; the Secretary of the Treasury's approval was necessary to make the change. Franklin MacVeagh gave his permission on July 14, 1909, and not quite three weeks later, on August 2, 1909, the new coin was released to the public"[38].

"The original model bore Brenner's name. Before the coins were issued, however, the initials "VDB" were substituted because officials at the United States Mint felt the name was too prominent. After the coin was released, many protested the initials were too conspicuous and detracted from the design. Because the coin was in high demand, and making a change would have required halting production, the decision was made to eliminate the initials. They were restored in 1918 and found on the rim, just under the shoulder of Lincoln.[39]"

"More one-cent coins are produced than any other denomination, which makes the Lincoln cent a familiar item. This coin has weathered two world conflicts in its life span, one of which changed it materially because metals play a vital part in any war effort.[40]"

"The metal content consisted of 95 percent copper and 5 percent zinc. These metals were denied to the Mint for the duration of the war, making it necessary for the Mint to seek a substitute material. After much deliberation, even

---

[37] US Treasury website
[38] US Treasury website
[39] US Mint website
[40] US Mint website

including plastics, zinc-coated steel was chosen as the best in a limited range of suitable materials.

Production of the war-time cent for in the act of Congress gained approval on December 18, 1942. The expiration date of the authority expired on December 31, 1946. Low-grade carbon steel formed the base of these coins, to which a zinc coating .005-inch-thick was deposited on each side electrolytically as a rust preventative. The same size was maintained, but the weight was reduced from the standard 48 grains to 42 grains due to the use of a lighter alloy. Production commenced on February 27, 1943, and by December 31, 1943, the three Mint facilities had produced 1,093,838,670 of the one-cent coins. The copper released for the war effort was enough to meet the combined needs of 2 cruisers, two destroyers, 1,243 flying fortresses, 120 field guns, and 120 howitzers, or enough for 1.25 million shells for our big field guns.[41]"

"On January 1, 1944, the Mint adopted a modified alloy. The supply derived from expended shell casing, which melted, furnished a composition like the original, but with a faint tin trace. The weight of 48 grains restored the coin to the initial release origins.[42]"

"In honor of Lincoln's 150th birth anniversary, the reverse changed to encompass the Lincoln Memorial. Frank Gasparro, then Assistant Engraver at the Philadelphia Mint, designed the new "reverse" of the coin.
The imposing marble Lincoln Memorial provides the central motif, with the legends E Pluribus Unum and the UNITED STATES OF AMERICA completing the design,

---

[41] US Mint website
[42] US Mint website

together with the denomination. The initials "F.G." appear on the right, near the shrubs.[43]"

The composition of the coin was changed again in 1962. The coin content changed to 95 percent copper and 5 percent zinc, eliminating the tin. Congressional authority for the modification came from an Act of Congress approved on September 5, 1962.[44]

1982 Transitional Lincoln Cents

"Inflation in the late 1970s and early 1980s at double digits drove the price of copper up. In 1982, a decision to change the content of the one cent occurred.[45]"

"Since the value of the cent was, by then, more symbolic than real, the new issue needed to look exactly like the existing cents. Any alternative metal needed plating with either pure copper or a high-copper alloy[46]."

"The bronze-clad steel cents tested a few years earlier were not satisfactory, so further tests resumed during 1980-81. The solution included a zinc planchet with a thin copper coating. The zinc base was .992 zinc and .008 copper, the trace amount of copper being included to facilitate bonding of the copper plating.[47]"

"All planchets for the new cents were designated to be fabricated by outside vendors and delivered ready to coin. On July 22, 1981, the Ball Corporation of Greenville, Tennessee signed a contract to manufacture press-ready

---

[43] US Treasury department
[44] US Treasury department
[45] US Mint website
[46] US Mint website
[47] US Mint website

planchets to be delivered no later than November. Production of the copper-plated zinc cents was anticipated to begin in December using dies dated 1982. Since the new cents would not be available in large quantities for several months, the coining of brass cents was expected to continue throughout much of 1982.[48]"

"Just as the zinc industry today supports the coining of cents using its product, in 1981 the copper producers howled at the prospect of losing their lucrative market. A lawsuit filed in October of that year by the Copper & Brass Fabricators Council alleged the Treasury Department lacked the legal authority to change the composition of the "penny.[49]"

"The District of Columbia's U.S. District Court dismissed the suit, citing the Council lacked the legal authority to sue! The dismissal, affirmed by the U.S. Court of Appeals, closed the suit forever.[50]"

"Coining of the zinc cents commenced on January 7, 1982, at the West Point Mint. (Little remembered today is that this facility produced nearly a billion cents from 1974 to 1985. As these bear no mintmarks, they are indistinguishable from those made at Philadelphia.) Soon after that, Philadelphia undertook this coinage, too. Denver continued to produce solely brass cents until October 21, 1982. That was conversion day. After coining brass cents in the morning, an hour's suspension was affected during which time all the remaining brass cents and planchets were cleared away. The striking of zinc cents began. The first delivery of these from the Coining Division was made

---

[48] US Mint website
[49] US Mint website
[50] US Mint website

on the 27th. The San Francisco Mint struck nearly four million proof cents for collectors, but these were all the traditional composition. It was found that the underlying zinc broke through its thin copper plating under the repeated impressions given to proof coins. This problem was solved in 1983 and subsequent years by furnishing each proof planchet with a second copper plating. Oddly enough, San Francisco did mint 1,587,245 zinc cents for general circulation in 1982. Like those made at West Point, however, these bear no mintmarks.[51]"

The coin hobby enjoyed a real windfall when the U.S. Mint decided to make a significant revision to the cent's obverse master hub midway through 1982. It is much smaller date most easily recognizes the new hub, and these Small Date cents were first struck September 3. Ultimately, a total of seven different combinations of date size, Mint and composition were created for the circulating cent coinage in 1982. A 1982-D Small Date Brass cent was not manufactured. When one adds the 1982-S Large Date Brass proof cent to this mix, the result is a most memorable year for collectors.[52]

Shield Design 2010-

The following is an official notice released by the U.S. Mint concerning the new 2010 Lincoln Cents:
"The current Lincoln cent's reverse (tails side) design is typical of President Abraham Lincoln's preservation of the United States as a single and united country. It was required by Title III of Public Law 109-145, the Presidential $1 Coin Act of 2005. The obverse (heads) continues to bear the familiar Victor David Brenner likeness of President Lincoln that has appeared on the coin

---

[51] US Mint website
[52] NGC website

since 1909. The reverse features a union shield with a scroll draped across and the inscription *ONE CENT.*
The 13 vertical stripes of the shield represent the states joined in one compact union to support the federal government, represented by the horizontal bar above. The horizontal bar features the inscription *E PLURIBUS UNUM—"out of many, one"*—while the inscription *UNITED STATES OF AMERICA* is depicted along the upper rim of the coin. The union shield, which dates to the 1780s, was used widely during the Civil War. The shield is also featured on frescoes by Constantino Brumidi throughout the halls of the U.S. Capitol Building completed in the mid-19th century.[53]"

"The Secretary of the Treasury approved the reverse design for the coin after consultation with the U.S. Commission of Fine Arts and review by the Citizen's Coinage Advisory Committee.[54]"

These one-cent coins have a metallic content of 2.5 percent copper, balance zinc. They are issued for circulation in quantities sufficient to meet the demands of commerce. Numismatic (proof and uncirculated) versions are included in the United States Mint's annual product offerings."[55]

Release of the 2017 Lincoln cent with P mint mark

"According to **Tom Jurkowsky**, director of the **United States Mint's** Office of Corporate Communications, the 2017-P Lincoln cent was minted in recognition of the Mint's **225th anniversary** on April 2. The addition of the

---

[53] From PCGS coin facts by Ron Guth
[54] From PCGS coin facts by Ron Guth
[55] From PCGS coin facts by Ron Guth

"P" mintmark was an idea suggested by employees of the **Philadelphia Mint**. The coin was intentionally released without fanfare to gauge how long it would take before the public questioned the Mint about the authenticity of the novel 2017-P pennies. The mint-marked Philadelphia one-cent coins were shipped to Federal Reserve Banks in early January for distribution into general circulation."[56]

---

[56] By **Joshua McMorrow-Hernandez** for <u>CoinWeek.com</u>

Glossary
Rev. 02.09.2021smc

Abrasions – Scattered lines on the surface of a coin caused by scratches on the die.

ANA – American Numismatic Association. The ANA provides insights into coin collecting. Anyone can join ANA for a small fee.

ANACS – American Numismatic Association Certification Service

Annealing – The metal is softened to enable details to be minted on coins. Metal rods are annealed to make Mint dies.

Anvil Die – The bottom die is used to create the reverse on a coin.

Bar Die Break – A die break over the tops of the lettering on a coin appears like a bar.

BIE – A die break between the letters B and I in Liberty creates an irregular line of raised metal.

Blank – A raw planchet ready for striking.

Bonded Pair – Two or more blanks enter the minting chamber struck together as one piece.

Brass Colored - Improper mixing of plating alloys creates a bronze color on the surface of copper coins.

Broken Hub – A piece of the coin detail is missing from the hub, and consequently, the die made from the hub lacks the full detail.

Brilliant Uncirculated – A term used to describe a coin with no wear and surface luster.

Broad struck – The collar holding the planchet for striking is cracked or missing creating a coin wider than usual.

Brockage - A brockage is a Mint error, an early capped die impression where a sharp incused image has been left on the next coin fed into the coining chamber. Most brockages are partial; full brockages are rare and the most desirable form of the error.[57]

Broken Punch – A punch used to create a die is partially broken, resulting in missing details.

Cameo – A proof or proof-like coin with a frosty appearance.

Canceled Planchet – A minted coin not meeting the Mint's standard is crushed in the shape of a waffle.

Carbon Spot – The dark spots on the surface of a coin are caused by oxidation and poor storage.

Cleaned – A coin with an altered surface from cleaning.

Clashed Dies – Dies pressed together in the minting process with no planchet. Each die has portions of design details from the opposite die.

Clipped Planchet – A planchet blank missing part of the circumference. Clipped planchets vary in degree and type of error.

Collar – A metal die that positions a planchet between the dies, so the coin is minted as intended. Collars are considered the "third" die and are used to impart the edge markings to a coin.

Collar Break Vertical - When the collar cracks vertically, the coins minted show the lettering and numbers butted against the rim.

Collar Clash - A collar clash occurs when the striking die is not lined up correctly, and the die strikes the collar. The features on the collar, sometimes a reeded edge, is transferred to the die.

Collar Vibration - During the coin striking, the collar vibrates, the hammer die pushes the coin down toward the anvil die, creating a sloping outer ridge toward the center of the coin.

Contact Marks – Nicks, and dents on coins from coins or other objects.

Corrosion – Damage to a coin caused by the environment or chemicals applied to the surface.

---

[57] PCGS – PCGS website for "Lingo"

Counter Brockage - A previously struck coin and capped die is a counter brockage. The capped die strikes a coin already struck, and the obverse design is impressed into the cap. The result will be a design where the cap face will be an incuse.

Counterstamp – A coin stamped by a second source making an intentional impression on the coin.

DCAM – Deep cameo coin

Denomination – The face value of a coin or bill. The Lincoln cent denomination is one cent.

Die – A die is a punch that contains the design used to imprint on a planchet.

Defective Planchet – A defective planchet refers to a blank which was split, cracked, or missing pieces before the coining process.

Die Adjustment – The pressure used to Mint a coin is adjusted, resulting in faint details.

Die Break – Die breaks result from a hammer or anvil die breaking. During the stamping process, the break is filled in with metal under pressure, forming raised areas on the surface of the coin.

Die Cap - The term applied to an error in which a coin gets jammed in the coining press and remains for successive strikes, eventually forming a "cap" either on the upper or lower die. These are sometimes spectacular, with the "cap" often many times taller than a normal coin.[58]

Die Clash – Dies struck together without a blank, creating impressions of the opposite die, which transfers to subsequent coins' surfaces.

Die Crack – A crack in the die resulting in a raised metal line that could branch out on a coin's surface.

Die Cud – A area of raised smooth metal around the rim caused by a piece of the die that has broken away.

Die Cud Retained – A retained cud occurs when a piece of the die breaks but is held in place by the collar.

---

[58] PCGS – PCGS website for "Lingo"

Die Errors – Coins minted from dies that are damaged or accidentally modified.

Die Gouges - The material in the form of short, thick, raised lines or bumps. Die gouges are caused by a die that has been deeply scratched by foreign material.

Die Scratches (see Abrasions) - A series of raised lines on a coin's surface from debris or die tooling.

Die Wear – The intended details on the coin are not sharp or missing.

DDO – Doubled die obverse

DDR –Doubled die reverse.

DMM – Doubled mintmark.

Doubled Die – A distinct doubling of the design on a coin created from dies doubled from the hub.

Double-Struck – A coin trapped in the collar struck a second time.

Extended Rim - An extended rim occurs with a deep strike on the coin. Slight tilting of the coin during the minting process creates a thin rim with a groove inside the rim.

FB – Full bands – The designation for Mercury dimes with full uninterrupted lies on the faces.

FBL – Full bell lines – The designation for Franklin halves with complete detail on the Liberty bell.

FH – Standing liberty quarters with full details on the head of the portrait.

Filled Dies – Dies that become filled with debris blocking the design details from being transferred to the coin.

Finned Rim – A coin minted with an extended rim missing metal fill. The fin on the rim is thin and extends part of the way around the coin.

Flip Over Strike – A coin jammed in the minting chamber is struck, flips over, and struck again with the opposite die.

Fold Over Strike – A coin not fully ejected in the minting chamber is struck again, crushing the coin.

Foreign Planchet – A planchet intended for mintages of Foreign county.

Flow lines – Lines on the surface of the coin caused by the metal spreading during striking.

FS – Full step designation for Jefferson nickels

Hammer Die – The die used to Mint the obverse design.

Hub – The punch used to create the design dies for minting coins. The design is the opposite of the actual image.

Hub Error – When a piece of the hub breaks off, the dies created from the hub are missing the detail.

Improperly Annealed – Planchets that are not properly softened for minting. The minted coins often appear with a red tint.

Indent – Another planchet enters the minting chamber and crushes into the minted coin, creating a deep impression.

Inverted Mintmark - A mintmark placed on a working die upside down.

Key Coin – The most valuable coin in a series

Lamination – A defective planchet is minted, and then the defective portion falls away.

Lamination Retained – The defective portion of the coin peels from the surface of the coin but remains on the coin.

Large Date – A coin release for a date with at least two different date sizes, one which is considered larger.

Machined Doubled – The striking die bounces slightly during the strike creating a thin raised area around the letters or numbers.

Master Die – A die produced from the original hub.

Master hub – A hub produced from a rubber mold design on hardened metal used to make minting dies.

Mated Pairs – Two planchets struck together in error. The coins separate and are boxed in the same container. The two separate coins are located as a pair.

Mintmark: The mintmark is a letter on most coins representing where the coins were minted.

D – Denver

S – San Francisco

P – Philadelphia (also no mintmark)

W – West Point

CC – Carson City

O – New Orleans

Mint Striking Errors – Errors created in the minting process.

Misalignment Dies - There are three dies, the hammer, the anvil, and the collar, designed to mint coins as intended. When the dies are not aligned correctly, the strike on the coin is not centered.

Misplaced Date (MPD)– The date is incorrectly positioned on the die.

Missing Details – Part of the design is not transferred to the coin properly.

Motto – The inscription on a coin such as IN GOD WE TRUST.

MS – Mint state grading system MS60 through MS70.

Mule – A mule is a coin minted with two different denominations on opposite sides.

Multiple Struck – A coin trapped in the collar and struck several times.

NG, No Grade – A coin with significant damage or other issues is not graded.

Numismatist – A person who studies and accumulates knowledge of coins.

Obverse – The front of a coin

Occluded Gas – Bubbles appear on the surface of the coin caused by gas trapped during the plating process.

Off Center – A coin struck on a blank that was not properly centered over the anvil, or lower, die.[59]

OMM – Over mintmark - A coin struck with a die repurposed with a different mintmark. In rare instances, branch mints returned dies with mintmarks punched into them. Examples include the 1938-D/S Buffalo nickel and the 1900-O/CC Morgan dollar.

---

[59] PCGS – PCGS website for "Lingo"

Overdate – The intended date is minted over another date not entirely removed from the die.

Partial Collar – A planchet fed into the minting chamber is stuck outside of the collar.

Partial Collar Tilted - A coin entering the minting chamber struck on an angle with a cracked or moving collar.

Phantom Mintmark – A mintmark not completely removed from a die faintly shows on coins.

PL – Proof like

Planchet – The blank used to mint coins.

PR - Proof

RB – Red Brown color

Repunched Mintmark – Doubling on a mintmark caused by not accurately punching over the existing mintmark.

Reverse Brockage - Similar brockage but with the portrait facing the opposite way.

Retained Collar Cud – The collar breaks in the minting process but does not split apart, resulting in an incomplete rim.

Rotated – Dies not aligned correctly, minting coins with the obverse and reverse not lined up correctly.

Rotated Mintmark – A mintmark placed on a die in a usual position.

RPM – Re-punched mintmark. The Mint takes dies of one mintmark and re-punches the die with another mintmark.

Saddle Strike – Saddle struck coins occur in a multi-press operation when the coin straddles two presses. Both presses stamp the coin while the coin bends between the dies in the shape of a saddle.

Sandwich Coin – The interior of a coin is one alloy covered by another alloy on both sides. Modern-day silver coins contain copper interiors with silver plating on both sides.

SMS – Special mint set

SP - Specimen

Split Planchet – A planchet that is missing a portion of metal on the surface.

Spread – The degree of doubling on a coin. Spreads are high, medium, and low.

Strike Through – Debris entering the minting chamber distorts the intended details on the coin.

Thin Planchet – All US denominations have tolerances for the thickness of the coin. When a planchet is thin or thick, the coin becomes lighter or heavier than intended.

Tilted Collar - A tilted collar strike occurs when a planchet enters the minting chamber on an angle and is struck by the hammer die pushing the coin flat. The result of this strike is a smooth outer surface lacking detail. There are varying degrees of part of the circumference of the coin missing details.

Tilted Mintmark – A mintmark hammered into a die at an angle, leaving the details thick on one side and thin on the other side.

Transitional – Coins struck with planchets not intended for a subsequent mintage. For example, a 1943 Lincoln cent struck on a bronze planchet. A 1983 Lincoln cent struck on a bronze planchet (no- zinc) is a transitional error.

Type one – The first intended issuance of a coin. For example, 1913 Buffalo nickel on a raised mound.

Type two – The Mint modified the design during the annual mintage of coins. The 1913 Buffalo nickel struck with a flat mound is a type II mintage.

Uniface - A coin planchet enters the minting chamber over a planchet already in the minting chamber. The planchets struck together, leave one side blank, and the other side with the intended details.

Unplated – A coin missing the plating layer exposing the inner core.

VAM – A numbering system created for silver dollar variations. VAM is short for the two people who logged silver dollar variances.

Variations - Variations are not mint errors in the technical sense. Differences in coins caused by creating hubs and dies not the same result in dates compared as large to small, wide to thin, etc.

Variety – Changes in the design of a coin particular to a mintage year.

Vertical Collar Break – A collar breaking vertically during the minting process, giving the coin a doubled rim.

Weakly Struck – A missing with lightly struck details due to worn or clogged dies.

Wheel marks – Faint highly polished lines on a coin caused by the rubber wheels in counting machines.

Whizzing – A process of using high-pressure water and brushes to clean the surface of a coin noted as whizzing. Whizzing reduces the value of a coin.

Wrong Metal – A metal alloy unintentionally used for the minting of coins such as brass.

Wrong Planchet – A planchet not intended for the mintage, such as a dime planchet minted in Lincoln cent dies.

[1] PCGS From the PCGS glossary
[2] PCGS – From the PCGS glossary
[3] PCGS – From the PCS glossary

References:

Photographs – Photographs are from the personal collection of the author, photographed at auctions, or validated pictures from the internet.

Error types – Error type descriptions are from years of collecting experience and interpretation is validated by the PCGS online glossary.

PCGS – As noted in this guide by footnotes.

The US Treasury Department – As footnoted in this guide

US Mint – Articles published by the US Mint

About the Author

I started collecting coins in 1962, and my passion for collecting has continued to grow to expand into error coins in the 1990s.

A 1909 VDB Lincoln cent was my inspiration for collecting. I was intrigued by the date and the large letters on the reverse of the coin, VDB. Before long, I purchased the Whitman blue folders for Lincoln cents and began to search for the dates and mint marked coins I could find. I bought all types of books and magazines to learn as much as I could about coins. These books helped me become an expert and enabled me to grade coins, even those I sent for encapsulation. My encapsulated coins have always come back as MS65 or higher, and I could not expect more.

I have never been able to locate the coins I was missing for my collection in circulation. I resorted to buying the coins I was missing to complete the set in the 1990s. It was in the 1990's I established SMCcoins LLC and began to sell online with a website. I attended every coin auction and estate sale to obtain coins to sell or add to my collection. In

1999, I gave up the website and reserved my efforts to write coin guides based on my 55 years of study.

The best method I determined for searching for dates I needed to fill my collection was to go to the local bank and obtain Lincoln cent rolls. After a year, I was able to fill the Lincoln cent folder from 1909 through 1963 will most of the coins. The only coins I was missing were most of the mint marked Lincoln cents dated before 1916. I had higher-end Lincoln cents for 1909, 1909 VDB, 1910, 1911, 1912, 1913, 1914, and 1915. I completed the Lincoln set from 1916, except for 1922, 1931-S, 1932, 1932-D, 1933, and 1933-D Lincoln cents. Lincoln cents with the San Francisco mint mark "S" were getting hard to locate in the early nineteen sixties. By the 1970s, S minted coins were near impossible to found.

The rarest coin from circulation I ever saw was a 1916-D Mercury Dime. My friend and I would search through coin rolls together in the early 1960s. We agreed to share our finds as we pooled our cash. Unfortunately, the thought of more money got the best of him, and he refused to share the profits.

Since the 1990s, I have found a 1950-D Jefferson nickel and scores of war nickels. My whole time was collecting nickels from the 1960s; I had never located a 1950-D. I searched through a box of nickels primarily for war nickels, which are scarce, but still can be found. I also discovered some error coins I sold to collectors.

To this day, I search through change and rolls of Lincoln cents with the hope of finding an error coin or a rare wheat cent that was hidden away for years. I sell error coins on the internet I locate from circulation or collections. I have found some exciting errors such as a cent minted on brass,

a 1983 Lincoln cent with no copper plating, many coins
with cracked dies, and one of my favorites, a Lincoln cent
with the reverse partially stamped on the front of the coin
(die clash).

I still meet people who have coins they want to be
appraised or sold. I do not buy collections, but I do sell the
coins for them. The most extensive collection I have ever
sold was for $30,000. Recently, a doctor came to me with a
bag of coins he had for years. He told me a coin dealer
offered him $400 for the lot. I looked at the coins and told
him I could get him $1200, and I would keep the rest. I
made $600.

In 2017, I met with a person who had three coins. The first
was a 1794 half dollar I appraised for $44,000. The second
coin was a 1911-D five-dollar gold piece, which I valued at
$5,000. The third coin was a chain cent dated 1793, was not
in the best shape; however, I valued this coin at $5,000. My
advice was to get all three of these coins encapsulated by
PCGS as soon as possible. From experience, encapsulating
a coin increases its value because collectors trust the
authenticity and the grading system from the encapsulation
services.

During the 1960s, collecting from circulation was fun since
countless numbers and types of coins were available. In the
1960s, Lincoln's cents were dated from 1909, Buffalo
nickels, Mercury dimes, Standing Liberty quarters, and
Walking Liberty half dollars. Occasionally, a silver dollar
could be found.

In the 1980s and 1990s, buying and selling coins allowed
me to complete many collections.
By 2000, I turned my attention to error coin collecting, and
I wrote my first coin guide of error coins, inspired by the

increasing numbers of error coins we offered at auctions. Over time I have been adding Lincoln cent error coins to my collection.

It takes a year of research to add to this book. I am dedicated to presenting the most accurate information. If you see or suspect an error in this book, please contact me. I hope you enjoy this book. If you have any questions, feel free to contact me at McDonald.Stan@comcast.net.

Grammar and Spelling edited by Grammarly – www.gramerly.com

Books written and offered by Stan McDonald

Lincoln Cent Error Coin Guide 2021 – color edition
2021 US Error Coin Guide
2021US Error Coin Guide – color edition
History of United States Coins – revised 2019
Jefferson Nickel Error Coin Guide 2020

References

Cannot find what you are looking for?
Try these SMC approved sites:
http://doubleddie.com/828970.html
http://lincolncentresource.com/doubledies/doubledies.html
http://varietyvista.com/CONECA%20Master%20Listings.htm
https://www.pcgs.com/news/1958-doubled-die-lincoln-cent-remains-elusive

Appendix A - Doubled Die Classifications

Class I Doubled Die – A class one doubled die relates to a 1955 or a 1969-S Lincoln cent, doubled. When reworking a die to the hub, the die is slightly rotated to the left or right, creating doubling the letters and numbers.

Class II Doubled Die – Class two doubled die shows the strongest doubling toward the coin's rim or doubling toward the center of the coin.

Above is "GOD" class II doubled die

Class III Doubled Die – When a die is impressed into a different working hub for the same mintage year - the results show doubling in the die differences. In 1960, there were dies producing large dates and small dates.

The 1960-D above is a small over a large date

Class IV Doubled Die - A Class IV doubled die occurred when the dies were made by a sequence of hubbing with an annealing process in between. The centers of the die and the hub are not aligned. Doubling is on all lettering and numbering on the coins. All coins dated 1998 and before used this process.

1982 Class IV doubled die.

Class V Doubled Die

Class V doubled die shows doubling to the right or the left around the coin with a widespread, into a medium spread, and finally a minor spread. For example, Liberty will have minor doubling while the date on the other side of the coin is wide-spread doubled.

Widespread

Medium spread

Minor spread

Class VI Doubled Die

Class six doubled die occurs when the letters or numbers on the coin are extra thick and may even slope downward. The

1973 Lincoln cent pictured is a class VI. Notice the line on the top photograph is aligned with the highest letter "E" and the photograph below is aligned with most of the tops of the letters.

2019

The numbers in the date are thicker than a typical strike. The Lincoln cent dated 2019 is an excellent example of a doubled die class VI.

Class VII Doubled Die

Class VII doubled die is the result of the mint modifying a hub to make a design change. For example, a two was removed from a hub and replaced by a three, but some of the two's details remained visible; the coins minted would be a "three over two." An example is 1942 over 1 Mercury dime.

An example of a class VII doubled die "2" over "4"

Class VIII Doubled Die

A class eight doubled die occurs when the hub is tilted, and a working die is made from this hub. The error shows a small doubling of letters in the form of a bump or a curve of raised material around the numbers and/or letters.

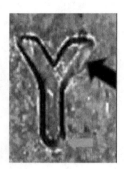

Appendix B - Reference for Denver Mintmarks 1970-2019

The US Mint changes the style of the Denver mintmark frequently. The photographs are from a brilliant uncirculated collection of Lincoln cents.

Variations of the Denver mintmark may occur in the year of minting from the mint preparing several dies, which are not precisely the same. Some of the mint variations are minute and detected only with a magnifying glass or microscope.

Each Lincoln cent mintage year dated from 1970 through 2019 is shown below. The photographs are to scale.

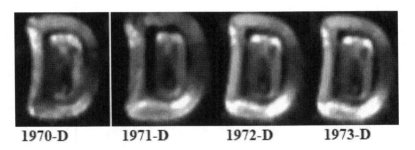

| 1970-D | 1971-D | 1972-D | 1973-D |

1970-1973 The D has sharp slopes with a small opening, which gets quickly filled with metal during the striking process. The 1970 and 1971 mintmarks are slightly different from 1972 and 1973, which are identical.

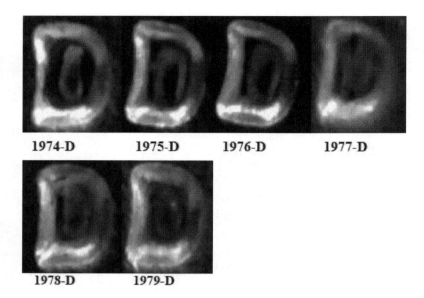

1974-D   1975-D   1976-D   1977-D

1978-D   1979-D

The mintmarks for the 1974-D through 1979-D have a wider inner opening. The slope of the D is smoother than the 1973-D mintage and the bottom of the D is thicker. The D mintmarks are larger in the series.

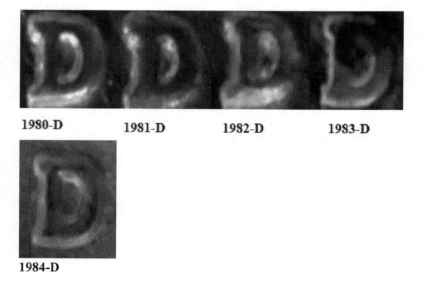

1980-D   1981-D   1982-D   1983-D

1984-D

The mintmarks for the 1980D through 1984-D changed to a smaller D with thicker sides, a smaller opening, and tails added to the top and bottom.

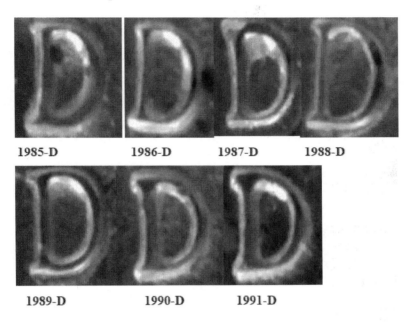

| 1985-D | 1986-D | 1987-D | 1988-D |

| 1989-D | 1990-D | 1991-D |

In 1985, the US Mint created die sets with the largest D on a Lincoln cent in history. Many coins have a large inner opening with thin outer lines. These coins are noticeable visually when comparing to other dates.

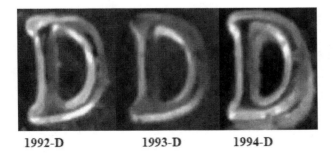

| 1992-D | 1993-D | 1994-D |

Although like the previous mint range of Denver strikes, the 1992-D, 1993-D, and 1994-D have thicker lettering.

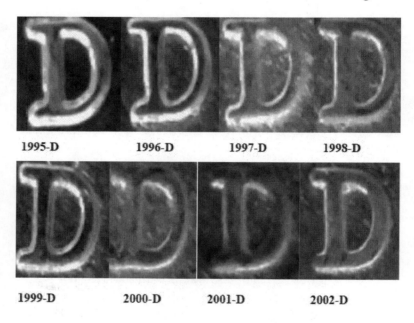

| 1995-D | 1996-D | 1997-D | 1998-D |

| 1999-D | 2000-D | 2001-D | 2002-D |

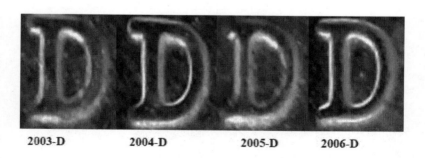

| 2003-D | 2004-D | 2005-D | 2006-D |

2007-D

The Denver mintages dated 1995-D through 2007-D have thick lettering and longer tails on the D from the previous range. Some examples in this range of mintages have a flat letter such as the 2007-D above.

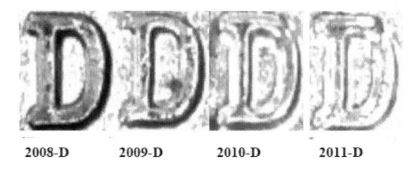

2008-D   **2009-D**   **2010-D**   **2011-D**

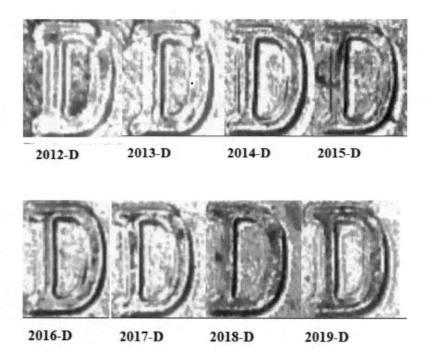

| 2012-D | 2013-D | 2014-D | 2015-D |

| 2016-D | 2017-D | 2018-D | 2019-D |

A major change in the design of the mintmark resulting in most coins appearing to be doubled. The mintmarks are not doubled but rather machine doubling. Many of these dated coins have flat D's with the letter ranging in thickness from one side of the mintmark to the other.

The BU sample of the 2019-D has a strong doubling effect, but collectors need to understand any doubling requires the doubling to be of the same height.

Rev 02.09.2021

Made in the USA
Columbia, SC
26 December 2021